THE
PSALMS

THE
PSALMS

LUIGI GIUSSANI

Translated by
Father William Vouk III

A Crossroad Book
The Crossroad Publishing Company
New York

The Crossroad Publishing Company
16 Penn Plaza, 481 Eighth Avenue
New York, NY 10001

First published as *Che cos'è l'uomo perché te ne curi?* Copyright ©
2000 by Edizioni San Paolo, Cinisello Balsamo (Milano).

English translation copyright © 2004 by the Crossroad Publishing
Company.

Translation and numbering of the Psalms is taken from the Revised
Standard Version, Catholic Edition, Princeton, N.J.: Scepter, 1966.

Printed in the United States of America

Library of Congress Cataloging-in-Publication Data

Giussani, Luigi.
[Che cosa e l'uomo perche te ne curi? English]
The Psalms / Luigi Giussani ; translated by William Vouk III.
p. cm.
Includes bibliographical references.
ISBN 0-8245-2124-2 (alk. paper)
1. Bible. O.T. Psalms – Meditations. I. Title.
BS1430.54.G5813 2004
223'.206 – dc22

                                                    2003026986

1 2 3 4 5 6 7 8 9 10   10 09 08 07 06 05 04

CONTENTS

PREFACE

THE MEMORY OF
THE COVENANT

We can understand Christian experience only with difficulty if we are unwilling to relive the history of the people of Israel, in all its aspects and in all its drama. Saint Paul asserts that the story of Israel is a pedagogical preparation for Christ. In fact, through the Hebrew people, the divine pedagogy aims to teach man that God is one, that He is creator, and that He realizes His mysterious plan by choosing a point in time, a point in space, and a small group of people. He chooses a people — ephemeral and fragile though they may be, yet certain of the covenant of the Lord — with a certainty that goes beyond any human limitations arising from original sin.

The Psalms are the form of dialogue defined by God Himself for His relationship with the people He has chosen. Anyone who recites them today takes on a Hebrew character, defined by a longing for fulfillment that arose in human history in a way that cannot be found in any other form of religious experience. The chief rabbi of Rome once remarked that while Christians want to bring man to Heaven, Jews want to bring God to Earth.[1]

It is precisely because of our approach that Christians feel ourselves to be brothers of the Jews. In the face of Jewish history there exists no vibration of human conscience that is kindlier and humbler — as if it were begging pardon of those who have borne *pondus diei et aestus,* that is, of those who have borne the weight of history — or more peaceful in affirming the fulfillment, which has already happened, of the prophecy for the entire universe in the Jew, Jesus of Nazareth, dead and risen.[2]

God has entered the reality of ancient Israel as a companion who determines the meaning of a path that has included both fidelity and betrayal, always showing Himself to be the Lord of history. The sweep of the Psalms tells this history with the evocative power of poetic song.

The Psalm represents the man with whom God has established the ancient covenant, to whom God has

1. See E. Toaff and A. Elkann, *Essere ebreo* (Milan: Bompiani, 1994), 40.

2. L. Giussani, "Noi siamo degli ebrei," *La Repubblica,* January 2, 1999, 13.

anticipated His coming — and so it is preparatory, an unfolding. One who does not read the Psalms does not understand the death and resurrection of Christ. But the sacraments are the cornerstone, particularly the Eucharist. When the priest at Mass says, "Blessed are you, Lord God of all creation, through your goodness we have this bread to offer, which earth has given and human hands have made," it is not just that bread: it is us. As the bread and the wine are the material of the presence of Christ as individual, so our flesh and our bones, our thoughts and our feelings are the bread and the wine, the material that is sensible in reality, in the sacrament of His mystical body, of Him in His fullness. When the priest extends his hands over the offerings at the beginning of the *Sanctus,* he extends them over all the people at Mass, so that they may become body and blood of Christ, so that the Word may become flesh and dwell in them. The ancient covenant is fulfilled.

THE
PSALMS

I

WHAT IS MAN THAT THOU ART MINDFUL OF HIM?
Psalm 8

O LORD, *our Lord,*
how majestic is thy name in all the earth!
Thou whose glory above the heavens is chanted
by the mouth of babes and infants,
thou hast founded a bulwark because of thy
     foes,
to still the enemy and the avenger.
When I look at thy heavens, the work of thy
     fingers,
the moon and the stars which thou hast
     established;
what is man that thou art mindful of him,
and the son of man that thou dost care for him?
Yet thou hast made him little less than God,
and dost crown him with glory and honor.

Thou hast given him dominion over the works
*   of thy hands;*
thou hast put all things under his feet,
all sheep and oxen,
and also the beasts of the field,
the birds of the air, and the fish of the sea,
whatever passes along the paths of the sea.
O LORD, *our Lord,*
how majestic is thy name in all the earth!

The time will come as we pray when we feel our
heart and our head opening wide as we understand
the words we are saying. The Psalms tell the story of
man, of man as *man,* with all his feelings, no matter
how contradictory. For there is nothing that can be
said to us or asked of us that does not pierce our
humanity.

O LORD, *our Lord, how majestic is thy name in*
all the earth! Thou whose glory above the heav-
ens is chanted [beyond what is visible, your glory
is chanted] *by the mouth of babes and infants, thou*
hast founded a bulwark because of thy foes, to still
the enemy and the avenger. The mouths of babes and
infants do not feel the struggle that exists between
the word of God, the revelation of God, the presence of God, and its enemies. But if the adult retains
the mouth of babes and infants, then he understands

God and His power in his struggle with his enemies. He feels it within himself. He feels the problem
of awareness, that is, the relationship between oneself and reality. As one understands awareness, so
he understands the relationship between himself and
reality. We could say, "With the simplicity we defend
by our maturity, You affirm Your power over Your
enemies."

*When I look at thy heavens, the work of thy
fingers, the moon and the stars which thou hast established; what is man* [What on earth is man?] *that
thou art mindful of him, and the son of man that
thou dost care for him?* But it is this — pardon me —
that I find myself saying every time I have to go to
do things when I need to be helped, because for old
men that's the way it is! But for the child, this is
not a suffering, a sacrifice for the ideal, that is, for
the meaning of what he does. "There is no ideal for
which we can sacrifice ourselves": there is no meaning of life that we can undertake, because everything
that is said in the modern mentality as such is a
falsehood.

Yet thou hast made him [this man] *little less than
the angels* [little less than Yourself: "the angels"
is a biblical formula for "manifestation of God"],
and dost crown him with glory and honor. Not just
kings or presidents, not heads of state or university

professors; God has crowned every "I" with glory and honor. Others must look upon him according to this dignity, however small or broken a man may be. Why has God done this? Because *thou hast given him dominion over the works of thy hands,* dominion over reality, over the universe. This is the recapitulation of everything that can be said about history: *thou hast put all things under his feet.*

The degradation of man is born right here. Sensing himself as made with this power, man degrades everything. "I am the measure of all things," they will say of reason, confusing reason with a presumption of theirs, that science is against the Church. Science is against the Church when it is not science, but a preconception that throws itself against the ecclesial reality and against what God says.

Within this Psalm lies the definition of the meaning of man's life — his relationship with the one who creates him.

The whole cosmos reaches for a certain point of evolution, at which it becomes self-awareness: that point is called "I." The "I" is self-awareness of the world, of the cosmos, and of oneself. The cosmos is the context in which the relationship with God, with the Mystery, lives.

The Psalmist asks, "Lord, what on earth is man that you keep him in mind, that you remember him?" Among all the beasts and little creatures of the cosmos, man is one-hundredth, a thousandth, a ten-thousandth. But the greatness of man, the honor and glory of man, lies in the fact that man, the individual man, is in relationship with the infinite. To live what man is, to realize his person, man must grasp everything that God has done. Happiness is the final end of this process, the process of penetrating the eternal.

Sooner or later, one begins to say this eighth Psalm of David every day. *and perhaps even to live?*

I Shall Be Satisfied
with Your Presence
Psalm 17

They close their hearts to pity;
with their mouths they speak arrogantly.
They track me down; now they surround me;
they set their eyes to cast me to the ground.
They are like a lion eager to tear,
as a young lion lurking in ambush.
Arise, O LORD! Confront them, overthrow
  them!
Deliver my life from the wicked by thy sword,
from men by thy hand, O LORD,
from men whose portion in life is of the world.
May their belly be filled with what thou hast
  stored up for them;
may their children have more than enough;
may they leave something over to their babes.

> *As for me, I shall behold thy face in*
>   *righteousness;*
> *when I awake, I shall be satisfied with beholding*
>   *thy form.* (Ps. 17:10–15)

Is there an expression which better than these verses
defines the new humanity to which we have been
called?

*May their children be filled with what thou hast
stored up for them; may they leave something over
to their babes. As for me, I shall behold thy face
in righteousness* [in the truth of things]; *when I
awake, I shall be satisfied with beholding thy form.*
When I awake on the other side of obscurity, on
the other side of appearances, nothing will interest me except for His presence. This is poverty. We
have understood nothing if poverty does not become
our love.

The instinct of poverty is the first tangible charac-
teristic of the new man. Poverty is born of charity.

We have seen this in the two verses: *May their belly
be filled with what thou hast stored up for them;
may their children have more than enough; may they
leave something over to their babes. As for me, I shall
behold thy face in righteousness; when I awake, I
shall be satisfied with beholding thy form.*

Abelard says, *Initium enim recedenti a Deo fastidium doctrinae est.* The beginning of resistance, of pulling oneself away from God, is annoyance at hearing the announcement, so that man inevitably waters it down. Let us be attentive to the fact that what we hear must become our daily bread.

3

I LOVE THEE, O LORD, MY STRENGTH
Psalm 18

I love thee, O LORD, my strength.
The LORD is my rock, and my fortress, and my
    deliverer,
my God, my rock, in whom I take refuge,
my shield, and the horn of my salvation, my
    stronghold.
I call upon the LORD, who is worthy to be
    praised,
and I am saved from my enemies.
The cords of death encompassed me,
the torrents of perdition assailed me;
the cords of Sheol entangled me,
the snares of death confronted me.
In my distress I called upon the LORD,
to my God I cried for help.

From his temple he heard my voice,
and my cry to him reached his ears. (Ps. 18:1–6)

I love thee, O LORD, my strength. The loving strength
that God communicates to us so that we can change
by embracing it, the most invasive presence in our life
and in all things, is called Spirit.

Normally, we pray — we repeat prayers, even
with emotion, being moved — but God is not the
dominant feeling.

Let us pray to the Holy Spirit that we may begin to
share in God's eternal creativity by changing, that we
may every evening notice a change that God makes
possible in us.

4

FOR THY NAME'S SAKE, O LORD, PARDON MY GUILT
Psalm 25

To thee, O LORD, I lift up my soul.
O my God, in thee I trust, let me not be put to
shame;
let not my enemies exult over me.
Yea, let none that wait for thee be put to shame;
let them be ashamed who are wantonly
treacherous.
Make me to know thy ways, O LORD;
teach me thy paths.
Lead me in thy truth, and teach me,
for thou art the God of my salvation;
for thee I wait all the day long.
Be mindful of thy mercy, O LORD,
and of thy steadfast love, for they have been
from of old.

*Remember not the sins of my youth, or my
        transgressions;
according to thy steadfast love remember me,
for thy goodness' sake, O LORD!
Good and upright is the LORD;
therefore he instructs sinners in the way.
He leads the humble in what is right,
and teaches the humble his way.
All the paths of the LORD are steadfast love and
        faithfulness,
for those who keep his covenant and his
        testimonies.
For thy name's sake, O LORD,
pardon my guilt, for it is great.* (Ps. 25:1–11)

Lead me in Your faithfulness; be my instructor, for You are my God. All those who wait for You will not be disappointed. *Let not my enemies exult over me. Yea, let none that wait for thee be put to shame.* I have waited for you day and night, because *good and upright is the LORD; therefore he instructs sinners in the way.*

When I talk about confession, I say that contrition and the firm purpose of amendment do not consist so much in the feeling of sorrow, or in a decision, because if we were capable of that, if we could do it on our own, the grace of the sacrament would be

Sacrament of Confession

useless. ✻ The sacrament always leads us back to the essence of the questions; it is made up of the essential: confession is a cry to God that He change me, because I am not capable of changing myself. It is the miracle of conversion.

Our hope is not in man, or in our doings, or in the refuges we build ourselves, or in the situation we finally reach to become creative, but in this thing that is so tremendously present that it challenges anything that others can promise us, in this thing that is God.

It is only the Spirit that can build the reign of God on earth, but we become the living stones. We build a new and indestructible event, the Church of God in history according to an irreducible contribution, and we do this to the degree that we place the certainty and energy of our existence in recognizing what has happened — to the degree that our entire ethic adheres to this form.

Psalm 131 says, "O LORD, my heart is not lifted up, my eyes are not raised too high."[1] We have depleted this original clarity; we empty it with every "but" and "if," with the daily push and pull, with the constant search for the exception and objection to God, with our constant demand for what we want. We have been told many times that we are children

---

1. Psalm 131:1. See text and commentary on page 146.

in the hands of Him who makes us. This child, this being has been created so that it might collaborate in the plan of the Father, in the plan of the reign of God, in the plan of Christ.

For thy name's sake, O LORD, pardon my guilt, for it is great. This *name* is the sign of the power the Lord uses to realize His plan in the world and in history. All my human hope in the salvation of Christ has grown because of my perception of being a sinner: *Pardon my guilt.* God's pardon requires all His strength, all His power, to turn me, a sinner, to one who gives glory to Him.

Where is there a more open definition of change than this?

5

MY HEART SHALL NOT FEAR
Psalm 27

The LORD is my light and my salvation;
whom shall I fear?
The LORD is the stronghold of my life;
of whom shall I be afraid?
When evildoers assail me,
uttering slanders against me,
my adversaries and foes,
they shall stumble and fall.
Though a host encamp against me,
my heart shall not fear;
though war arise against me,
yet I will be confident.
One thing have I asked of the LORD,
that will I seek after;
that I may dwell in the house of the LORD
all the days of my life,

to behold the beauty of the LORD,
and to inquire in his temple.
For he will hide me in his shelter
in the day of trouble;
he will conceal me under the cover of his tent,
he will set me high upon a rock.
And now my head shall be lifted up
above my enemies round about me;
and I will offer in his tent sacrifices with shouts
        of joy;
I will sing and make melody to the LORD.
Hear, O LORD, *when I cry aloud,*
be gracious to me and answer me!
Thou hast said, "Seek ye my face."
My heart says to thee, "Thy face, LORD, *do I*
        seek."
Hide not thy face from me.
Turn not thy servant away in anger,
thou who hast been my help.
Cast me not off, forsake me not, O God of my
        salvation!
For my father and my mother have forsaken
        me,
but the LORD *will take me up.*
Teach me thy way, O LORD;
and lead me on a level path
because of my enemies.

Give me not up to the will of my adversaries;
for false witnesses have risen against me,
and they breathe out violence.
I believe that I shall see the goodness of the
  L<small>ORD</small>
in the land of the living!
Wait for the L<small>ORD</small>; *be strong, and let your heart*
  take courage;
yea, wait for the L<small>ORD</small>!

Though a host encamp against me, my heart shall not fear; though war arise against me, yet I will be confident. Where is this certainty in us? Whatever forgetfulness, weakness, or incoherence may exist in us, it is constantly conquered by this certainty. It lies at the bottom of our heart, in that place where the Lord has descended. For after his death He descended into the bowels of the earth, which means that he descended to the root of our being.

Before it shows itself in us, it may be that a long road, unforeseen by us, will have to be traveled. But this certainty has as its root the entrusting of ourselves to the Lord, the recognition that we belong to Him. Where in us is this awareness of belonging?

One thing have I asked of the L<small>ORD</small>, *that will I seek after; that I may dwell in the house of the* L<small>ORD</small>

*all the days of my life, to behold the beauty of the
LORD, and to inquire in his temple.*

*Hear, O LORD, when I cry aloud, be gracious to
me and answer me! Thou hast said, "Seek ye my
face." My heart says to thee, "Thy face, LORD, do
I seek." Hide not thy face from me. Turn not thy
servant away in anger, thou who hast been my help.*
Where is this faithfulness, this certainty of our belonging, even in the midst of the devastation of our
wretchedness?

"Do not let your hearts be troubled," we have
heard, "believe in me" (see John 14:1), trust in me.
*The LORD is my light and my salvation; whom shall
I dread? The LORD is the stronghold of my life; of
whom shall I be terrified?* Where in our day and age
is this security, this humble boldness, this memory?

We do not pass from death to life without being
sure of the memory that: *The LORD is my light and
my salvation; the LORD is the stronghold of my life.
Teach me thy way, O LORD. Wait for the LORD; be
strong, and let your heart take courage; yea, wait for
the LORD!* This is what the Jews were accustomed
to say. This Lord was in the climate and air of the
people, in the empty mysteriousness of the temple,
in the fragile feeling of the soul. But to us it has
been revealed that God has become man — born of a
woman, made of flesh, and that He would be present

among us until the end of time. Where is this vitality and simplicity of faith in our houses? Who among us has said, even to himself, "He is among us"? It is not only forgetfulness; it is something more: a diminishment of faith, of the recognition of His presence. This is our sin, which finds its full expression in our lack of memory, and this empty space becomes taken up by "gods" — those things in which we have placed our trust — or our moods, the rebellion of wrath, or the facile hope that draws us every day into a frenetic volatility.

How do I see this forgetfulness play out in my own life? What is required to change? Is it required to change?

6

Look to Him,
and Be Radiant
Psalm 34

I will bless the LORD at all times;
his praise shall continually be in my mouth.
My soul makes its boast in the LORD;
let the afflicted hear and be glad.
O magnify the LORD with me,
and let us exalt his name together!
I sought the LORD, and he answered me,
and delivered me from all my fears.
Look to him, and be radiant;
so your faces shall never be ashamed.
This poor man cried, and the LORD heard him,
and saved him out of all his troubles.
The angel of the LORD encamps
around those who fear him, and delivers them.
O taste and see that the LORD is good!
Happy is the man who takes refuge in him!

O fear the LORD, *you his saints,*
for those who fear him have no want!
The young lions suffer want and hunger;
but those who seek the LORD *lack no good*
    thing. (Ps. 34:1–10)

I sought the LORD, *and he answered me, and de-*
livered me from all my fears. Look to him, and be
radiant; so your faces shall never be ashamed. This
poor man cried, and the LORD *heard him, and saved*
him out of all his troubles. Whatever difficulty we
may encounter on our path, only one thing is necessary: a posture of coherence — not as an expressive
capacity, nor even as actions (for that is the miracle
of the Spirit in our life), but rather as acceptance.

I sought the LORD, I seek the Lord: "When the
righteous cry for help, the LORD hears, and delivers
them out of all their troubles. The LORD is near to
the brokenhearted, and saves the crushed in spirit"
(Ps. 34:17–18). Not even error is a difficulty that can
stop you. When our difficulties, of whatever kind, are
capable of stopping us, of casting doubt upon our
path, it means that it is not the Lord we seek, but
what we love. And what we love and seek above all
is not the Lord.

7

I HAVE NOT SEEN
THE RIGHTEOUS FORSAKEN
Psalm 37

The LORD knows the days of the blameless,
and their heritage will abide for ever;
they are not put to shame in evil times,
in the days of famine they have abundance.
But the wicked perish;
the enemies of the LORD
are like the glory of the pastures,
they vanish — like smoke they vanish away.
The wicked borrows, and cannot pay back,
but the righteous is generous and gives;
for those blessed by the LORD shall possess the
        land,
but those cursed by him shall be cut off.
The steps of a man are from the LORD,
and he establishes him in whose way he delights;
though he fall, he shall not be cast headlong,

for the LORD *is the stay of his hand.*
I have been young, and now am old;
yet I have not seen the righteous forsaken
or his children begging for bread.
He is ever giving liberally and lending,
and his children become a blessing.
Depart from evil, and do good;
so shall you abide for ever.
For the LORD *loves justice;*
he will not forsake his saints.
The righteous shall be preserved for ever,
but the children of the wicked shall be cut off.
The righteous shall possess the land,
and dwell upon it for ever. (Ps. 37:18–29)

The wicked perish; the enemies of the LORD *vanish:* Such are the people that carry God's truth into the world, the scope of the action of God and Christ, that all the images of the God of Israel are warlike images. But then the warlike tone gives way to the tenderness of an intimacy: *The steps of a man are from the* LORD, *and he establishes him in whose way he delights; though he fall, he shall not be cast head-long, for the* LORD *is the stay of his hand. I have been young, and now am old; yet I have not seen the righteous forsaken.* Who are the righteous? The ones who ask God!

8

THEN I SAID,
"LO, I COME"
Psalm 40

I waited patiently for the LORD;
he inclined to me
and heard my cry.
He drew me up from the desolate pit,
out of the miry bog,
and set my feet upon a rock,
making my steps secure.
He put a new song in my mouth,
a song of praise to our God.
Many will see and fear,
and put their trust in the LORD.
Blessed is the man who makes the LORD his
      trust,
who does not turn to the proud,
to those who go astray after false gods!
Thou hast multiplied, O LORD my God,

> *thy wondrous deeds and thy thoughts toward*
>   *us;*
> *none can compare with thee!*
> *Were I to proclaim and tell of them,*
> *they would be more than can be numbered.*
> *Sacrifice and offering thou dost not desire;*
> *but thou hast given me an open ear.*
> *Burnt offering and sin offering thou hast not*
>   *required.*
> *Then I said, "Lo, I come;*
> *in the roll of the book it is written of me;*
> *I delight to do thy will, O my God;*
> *thy law is within my heart."* (Ps. 40:1–8)

Sacrifice and offering thou dost not desire [rites are not pleasing to you]; *but thou hast given me an open ear. Burnt offering and sin offering thou hast not required* [to purify me: organizational duty does not purify me, nor formal obedience]. *Then I said, "Lo, I come; in the roll of the book* [in the history of passing time] *it is written of me* to fulfill *thy will."*

It is because we do not call upon the Spirit that we are so obtuse; and the "house" (Ps. 40:1–8) becomes dark and its air takes on an odor of heaviness, so that one thinks he is breathing a mouthful of fresh air when he goes out the door and breathes in the tiresome air of our cities.

It is this freedom that must enter into daily action. You cannot put your freedom on hold; you cannot put yourself on hold.

The fervor of *delight to do thy will, O my God; thy law is within my heart* should be the dynamic of every day.

In God's law — His plan of communion, of alliance and familiarity with us — lies the consistency of the human person.

9

By This I Know That Thou Art Pleased with Me
Psalm 41

As for me, I said, "O Lord, be gracious to me;
heal me, for I have sinned against thee!"
My enemies say of me in malice:
"When will he die, and his name perish?"
And when one comes to see me, he utters empty
*   words,*
while his heart gathers mischief;
when he goes out, he tells it abroad.
All who hate me whisper together about me;
they imagine the worst for me.
They say, "A deadly thing has fastened upon
*   him;*
he will not rise again from where he lies."
Even my bosom friend in whom I trusted,
who ate of my bread, has lifted his heel
*   against me.*

But do thou, O LORD, be gracious to me,
and raise me up, that I may requite them!
By this I know that thou art pleased with me,
in that my enemy has not triumphed over me.
But thou hast upheld me because of my integrity,
and set me in thy presence for ever.

(Ps. 41:4–12)

The point of asking is the point where a person be-gins to turn, where he begins to break — because one cannot ask without beginning the renunciation of self. Without asking, desire remains vague and an-ticipation is confused with an expectation that things will change in accord with the preoccupations of our own imaginations.

The words of Psalm 41 tell us whether we have asked for a sign of loving piety and redemption: *By this I know that thou art pleased with me, in that my enemy has not triumphed over me.* This is the great-est challenge to the nobility and faithfulness of God. *But thou hast upheld me because of thy integrity.*

THOU ART MY KING
Psalm 44

We have heard with our ears, O God,
our fathers have told us,
what deeds thou didst perform in their days,
in the days of old:
thou with thy own hand didst drive out the
*   nations, but them thou didst plant;*
thou didst afflict the peoples, but them thou
*   didst set free;*
for not by their own sword did they win the
*   land,*
nor did their own arm give them victory;
but thy right hand, and thy arm,
and the light of thy countenance;
for thou didst delight in them.
Thou art my King and my God,
who ordainest victories for Jacob.
Through thee we push down our foes;

through thy name we tread down our assailants.
For not in my bow do I trust,
nor can my sword save me.
But thou hast saved us from our foes,
and hast put to confusion those who hate us.
In God we have boasted continually,
and we will give thanks to thy name for ever.

(Ps. 44:1–8)

For not by their own sword did they win the land,
nor did their own arm give them victory; but thy right
hand, and thy arm, and the light of thy countenance;
for thou didst delight in them.

The psalmist looks back on the long history that gave birth to his perspective on the world, to the meaning the world has for him. It was not the intelligence of his ancestors, but the light of the face of God Himself, the wisdom and the spirit of God that illuminated with true meaning what they looked upon — just as in the night, as Saint Peter says in one of his letters, one tries to catch sight of burning torches here and there (see 2 Pet. 1:19).

The Spirit of God made the Jewish people the undaunted, tenacious, and faithful proclaimers of the one God, *Jehovah,* pure Mystery. He is the Creator. The explanation for the world is in Him, and the end of the world, the purpose of the world, is Him.

This idea consolidated a whole people who arose through the ages from Abraham down to the psalmist. How was a tribe as small as it was, born of Abraham and his children, able to take on so many peoples in such a long journey and to conquer the richest land in the Middle East? Not with their sword (which they still used), not with their strength (which they still exerted), but with the right hand and arm of God!

What wonder there is in the miracle of this people, who arose from an invisible point in the distance, and grew up with such internal consistency.

It is not our intelligence that allows us to understand who God is, who Christ is, who Jesus is, or to understand that life draws meaning from Him and that the task of life is His glory. Even when it obscures itself, our intelligence does not obscure the truth of the words it speaks and the witness it finds itself committed to.

It is the light of His face, the light of the Spirit of God that makes our reality, which rises from an extremely distant point in history: that Man on the cross. Yet here we are now, speaking of Him. He has created a presence and launched His presence into time so that it unites us now, cries out to us now, stands before us now, and asks for us now.

It is not without reason that the demon is called lie, the "father of lies" (John 8:44), and the lie is confusion; it is a pitfall, as the Psalm says. In contrast, the ways of God are clear, like the road that stretches unobstructed as far as the eye can see. As the prophet Isaiah asks: "Behold, I am doing a new thing; now it springs forth, do you not perceive it?" (Isa. 43:19). Elsewhere Isaiah gives another comparison: "Behold, there is a new highway, do you not see it?" (Isa. 35:8). It is not a work we accomplish, but something given to our life.

We have heard with our ears, our fathers have told us, what deeds thou didst perform. In our life there is a witness more mature than our own, a vision of greater breadth and duration than ours.

11

THOU HAST MADE US
LIKE SHEEP FOR SLAUGHTER
Psalm 44

Yet thou hast cast us off and abased us,
and hast not gone out with our armies.
Thou hast made us turn back from the foe;
and our enemies have gotten spoil.
Thou hast made us like sheep for slaughter,
and hast scattered us among the nations.
Thou hast sold thy people for a trifle,
demanding no high price for them.
Thou hast made us the taunt of our neighbors,
the derision and scorn of those about us.
Thou hast made us a byword among the
*   nations,*
a laughingstock among the peoples.
All day long my disgrace is before me,
and shame has covered my face,

at the words of the taunters and revilers,
at the sight of the enemy and the avenger.

(Ps. 44:9–16)

If the beginning of Psalm 44 clearly proclaimed *Thou art my King and my God, who ordainest victories for Jacob* [for Israel, the people of God], the second part of the Psalm paints a desolate picture.

Thou hast cast us off and abased us: the mood we so often cast ourselves into is like a land ravaged and burned by our enemies, put to fire and sword. *Thou hast not gone out with our armies; thou hast made us ... a laughingstock among the peoples.* All of this has happened to us.

All day long my disgrace is before me. These words resound in us: the indignity of living, the total absence of any possibility of fame, that is, of having an impact on our existence or the existence of others, a feeling of not belonging in the greatness of history (both the history of a people and our personal history).

The fall we had yesterday, which falls back on us today, will make it easy to slip into dissonance and disgrace if something does not intervene. And again it is God, Jesus, who must intervene. Do intervene, Lord, so that this disgrace and this shame do not become the incentive for scorn on the part of the world, which, instead of finding in us a witness, an inducement to believe, finds a reason for not believing.

12

ROUSE THYSELF!
WHY SLEEPEST THOU, O LORD?
Psalm 44

All this has come upon us,
though we have not forgotten thee,
or been false to thy covenant.
Our heart has not turned back,
nor have our steps departed from thy way,
that thou shouldst have broken us in the place
       of jackals,
and covered us with deep darkness.
If we had forgotten the name of our God,
or spread forth our hands to a strange god,
would not God discover this?
For he knows the secrets of the heart.
Nay, for thy sake we are slain all the day long,
and accounted as sheep for the slaughter.
Rouse thyself! Why sleepest thou, O Lord?
Awake! Do not cast us off for ever!

Why dost thou hide thy face?
Why dost thou forget our affliction and
    oppression?
For our soul is bowed down to the dust;
our body cleaves to the ground.
Rise up, come to our help!
Deliver us for the sake of thy steadfast love!
                    (Ps. 44:17–26)

All this [dislocation, derision, disgrace] *has come upon us, though we have not forgotten thee, or been false to thy covenant.* Why do You act in this way? Why have You abandoned me? I have not forgotten You; I have not betrayed Your covenant; I have not turned back my heart; my steps have not strayed from Your path. And so I cry out, *Rouse thyself! Why sleepest thou, O Lord?* Thus we are all the day long as if *slain . . . , and accounted as sheep for slaughter.*

This third part of Psalm 44 describes the moment of asking, of begging.

Awake! Do not cast us off for ever! We are confused, distracted, negative, yet we have not forgotten You; we have stayed on Your way and our steps have not strayed from Your path.

Why does God allow the world to overpower us so that we must follow in our actions as slaves of the common mentality? Yet we have not adored what the world adored, even when our hearts rose up to it. *Why dost thou hide thy face? Why dost thou forget* this *affliction and oppression* of mine, this bowing down in the dust, as my body *cleaves to the ground? Rise up*, come to my aid, save me *for the sake of thy steadfast love.* For there is no other way; in the worst of moments there is no other way.

It is up to the Lord to make us cry out, *Rouse thyself! Why sleepest thou, O Lord?* or to lead us to write, "I am well, because I am always accompanied by the certainty that He possesses me." What greatness has been assigned to every moment of our life! "I am His for eternity, which for me is lived out in the instant." Living eternity in the instant is what gives our days strength, purpose, greatness, and fascination.

The beginning of eternal happiness is exactly at this point, at the point when we ask the Lord to reveal Himself and not cast us off forever, to show His face to us. We ask God not to forget the affliction and oppression that we are always enduring, by the very nature of faith in the world; not to forget that we are bowed down in the dust, that our body cleaves to the ground. Only God can make us get up and walk again in the darkness of the world, where all around is death. Only God can make us walk in the light and, as He said before He died, in joy (see John 15:10–11).

13

WHEN GOD RESTORES THE FORTUNES OF HIS PEOPLE
Psalm 53

The fool says in his heart,
"There is no God."
They are corrupt, doing abominable iniquity;
there is none that does good.
God looks down from heaven upon the sons of
  men
to see if there are any that are wise, that seek
  after God.
They have all fallen away;
they are all alike depraved;
there is none that does good,
no, not one.
Have those who work evil no understanding,
who eat up my people as they eat bread,
and do not call upon God?
There they are, in great terror,

in terror such as has not been!
For God will scatter the bones of the ungodly;
*they will be put to shame, for God has rejected
    them.*
*O that deliverance for Israel would come from
    Zion!*
When God restores the fortunes of his people,
Jacob will rejoice and Israel be glad.

*O that deliverance for Israel would come from Zion!
When God restores the fortunes of his people, Jacob
will rejoice and Israel be glad.*

Those who have been carried off will be carried
back, and that which is not understood will be understood if there is trust in God and faithfulness to the
covenant.

Faithfulness to the covenant can also be understood this way: Lord, I err a thousand times a day,
and a thousand times a day I am sorry for my
error; but I do not abandon Your way, and I do not
renounce Your covenant.

14

I WILL TRUST IN THEE
Psalm 55

Give ear to my prayer, O God;
and hide not thyself from my supplication!
Attend to me, and answer me;
I am overcome by my trouble.
I am distraught by the noise of the enemy,
because of the oppression of the wicked.
For they bring trouble upon me,
and in anger they cherish enmity against me.
My heart is in anguish within me,
the terrors of death have fallen upon me.
Fear and trembling come upon me,
and horror overwhelms me.
And I say, "O that I had wings like a dove!
I would fly away and be at rest;
yea, I would wander afar,
I would lodge in the wilderness,

I would haste to find me a shelter
from the raging wind and tempest."
But I call upon God;
and the LORD *will save me.*
Evening and morning and at noon
I utter my complaint and moan,
and he will hear my voice.
He will deliver my soul in safety
from the battle that I wage,
for many are arrayed against me.
God will give ear, and humble them,
he who is enthroned from of old;
because they keep no law,
and do not fear God.
My companion has stretched out his hand
         against his friends,
he violated his covenant.
His speech was smoother than butter,
yet war was in his heart;
his words were softer than oil,
yet they were drawn swords.
Cast your burden on the LORD,
and he will sustain you;
he will never permit
the righteous to be moved.
But thou, O God, wilt cast them down
into the lowest pit;

men of blood and treachery
shall not live half their days.
But I will trust in thee. (Ps. 55:1–8, 16–23)

In the midst of the bedlam of life, in the midst of all our struggles and our tragic weaknesses, how do we overcome everything that comes against us?

Yea, I would wander afar, I would lodge in the wilderness, I would haste to find me a shelter from the raging wind and tempest. I want to escape, I want to withdraw. But no!

Cast your burden on the LORD, *and he will sustain you; he will never permit the righteous to be moved.* The Lord cannot permit your love and the search for His will in your life to be moved.

Behold, *I will trust in thee.* I do not flee. I trust in God.

15

IN THE DAY WHEN I CALL
Psalm 56

Be gracious to me, O God,
for men trample upon me;
all day long foemen oppress me;
my enemies trample upon me all day long,
for many fight against me proudly.
When I am afraid,
I put my trust in thee.
In God, whose word I praise,
in God I trust without a fear.
What can flesh do to me?
All day long they seek to injure my cause;
all their thoughts are against me for evil.
They band themselves together, they lurk,
they watch my steps.
As they have waited for my life . . .
Thou hast kept an account of my tossings;
put thou my tears in thy bottle!

Are they not in thy book?
Then my enemies will be turned back
in the day when I call.
This I know, that God is for me.
In God, whose word I praise,
in the LORD, *whose word I praise,*
in God I trust without a fear.
What can man do to me?
My vows to thee I must perform, O God;
I will render thank offerings to thee.
For thou hast delivered my soul from death,
yea, my feet from falling,
that I may walk before God
in the light of life. (Ps. 56:1–6, 8–13)

The poor man is the one who begs; the poor man is
the one who calls upon another. *Then my enemies
will be turned back in the day when I call. This I
know, that God is for me.* God has given me life, He
has let me live within His mystery, the mystery of His
Son; He has allowed me to encounter the presence of
His Son.

Man's enemy pushes him back toward nothingness.
But because man has been loved, and thus called,
being pushed back toward nothingness is always a lie
now, a renunciation. It is no longer a neutral deed. My
enemies are those who make me forget Christ, who

do not make me call upon Christ, who do not make me see His presence in the presence of everything.

Then my enemies will be turned back, not in the day when I think, feel, do, or say, but *in the day when I call.*

I think it should not be difficult for any one of us to sense the absolute and fascinating truth of these words about calling upon another. (Truth is always fascinating because it always lies in beauty.) If we look at ourselves when we call upon another, we see the poor man with riches, the inconstant one who finds a new steadfastness that is not his. We see ourselves made by a Presence, conceived of a Presence.

My enemies will be turned back in the day when I call: This leads us to what prayer must be: absolutely pure, the only purity in life. We understand that prayer is total asking, without reservation. Prayer does not ask for something we want, something we have thought of; rather, it asks of someone Other because of the impression that this Other makes upon us.

Calling upon Him is the purest thing there is. It corresponds with our perception that we wholly belong.

The child that we read of in Psalm 131 who is quieted in the arms of his mother,[1] in his human

---

1. See Psalm 131:2. Text and commentary on page 146.

reality, is nothing other than the act of asking. From the ontological point of view, the whole of nature cries out to God that He feed it; the whole of nature asks for being. The child in the Psalm is like man; in his abandonment, he wants his mother to take him in her arms and hold him close to her.

There is an ultimate horizon to this abandonment, namely, complete gratuitousness, even if it remain unconscious. *Then my enemies will be turned back in the day when I call:* they may return to their attack at any moment, yet *this I know, that God is for me.* This is the psychological content of an asking that fully and purely expresses the truth of our "I." It contains our awareness of the value of the fact that He has given us life, that He has let us know Him, that He has let us encounter Him and that He has desired us for Himself. "I remember the days of old, I meditate on all that thou hast done; I muse on what thy hands have wrought."[2] This passage from Psalm 143 is a commentary on Psalm 56. Imagine in contrast to the position of the one who "remembers and calls upon," someone asking of another, "How can you throw your life away like that?" This small-mindedness does not express the drama of our nothingness, and does not glorify God. If we are here

---

2. Psalm 143:5. Text and commentary on page 158.

to speak these words, and if we can get up in the morning and pray with the people He has brought close to us, it is because God is for us.

It is an exercise in wonder, of gratitude, to repeat in front of Him what Psalm 143 has recalled to us: "I remember the days of old; I meditate on all that thou hast done; I muse on what thy hands have wrought."

16

I WILL AWAKE THE DAWN!
Psalm 57

Be merciful to me, O God, be merciful to me,
for in thee my soul takes refuge;
in the shadow of thy wings I will take refuge,
till the storms of destruction pass by.
I cry to God Most High,
to God who fulfils his purpose for me.
He will send from heaven and save me,
he will put to shame those who trample
*   upon me.*
God will send forth his steadfast love and his
*   faithfulness!*
I lie in the midst of lions
that greedily devour the sons of men;
their teeth are spears and arrows,
their tongues sharp swords.
Be exalted, O God, above the heavens!
Let thy glory be over all the earth!

They set a net for my steps;
my soul was bowed down.
They dug a pit in my way,
but they have fallen into it themselves.
My heart is steadfast, O God,
my heart is steadfast!
I will sing and make melody!
Awake, my soul!
Awake, O harp and lyre!
I will awake the dawn!
I will give thanks to thee, O Lord, among the
    peoples;
I will sing praises to thee among the nations.
For thy steadfast love is great to the heavens,
thy faithfulness to the clouds.
Be exalted, O God, above the heavens!
Let thy glory be over all the earth! (Ps. 57:1–11)

My heart is steadfast, O God, my heart is steadfast! I will sing and make melody! Awake, my soul! Awake, O harp and lyre! I will awake the dawn!

This is the theme of every morning of the world: *I will awake the dawn!*

It is for this liveliness of heart that we must ask.

We must not be controlled by our mood, which is determined by a kind of force of gravity, like all things in this world. We never pray to Christ and we never think of Christ if we are not renewed. If something new does not break through, we either pray merely formally, or our prayer is ruled by our mood.

17

THOU ART MY FORTRESS
Psalm 59

Deliver me from my enemies, O my God,
protect me from those who rise up against me,
deliver me from those who work evil,
and save me from bloodthirsty men.
For lo, they lie in wait for my life;
fierce men band themselves against me.
For no transgression or sin of mine, O LORD,
for no fault of mine, they run and make ready.
Rouse thyself, come to my help, and see!
O my Strength, I will sing praises to thee;
for thou, O God, art my fortress.
My God in his steadfast love will meet me;
my God will let me look in triumph on my
    enemies.
But I will sing of thy might;
I will sing aloud of thy steadfast love in the
    morning.

> *For thou hast been to me a fortress*
> *and a refuge in the day of my distress.*
> *O my Strength, I will sing praises to thee,*
> *for thou, O God, art my fortress,*
> *the God who shows me steadfast love.*
>   (Ps. 59:1–4, 9–10, 16–17)

O my Strength, I will sing praises to thee, for thou, O God, art my fortress, the God who shows me steadfast love.

The one who rises up against us is the one who hurts our integrity. It is also the evil that has slipped inside of us. If we have told a lie, if we have shared in the lie of idolatry, or in the exaltation of the particular, of abject giving in, of disgraceful weakness, we are redeemed by this sudden entry of God Himself into our *fortress.* If we are victims of the lie (in Saint John sin is identified with the lie and is normally called lie; see John 8:44), then the fruit of this mercy is the eradication of our defect, of our lessening, of our idolatrous identification.

18

THOU HAST MADE THY PEOPLE SUFFER HARD THINGS
Psalm 60

O God, thou hast rejected us, broken our
    defenses;
thou hast been angry; oh, restore us.
Thou hast made the land to quake, thou hast
    rent it open;
repair its breaches, for it totters.
Thou hast made thy people suffer hard things;
thou hast given us wine to drink that has made
    us reel.
Thou hast set up a banner for those who fear
    thee,
to rally to it from the bow.
That thy beloved may be delivered,
give victory by thy right hand and answer us!
God has spoken in his sanctuary:
"With exultation I will divide up Shechem

and portion out the Vale of Succoth.
Gilead is mine; Manasseh is mine;
Ephraim is my helmet;
Judah is my scepter.
Moab is my washbasin;
upon Edom I cast my shoe;
over Philistia I shout in triumph."
Who will bring me to the fortified city?
Who will lead me to Edom?
Hast thou not rejected us, O God?
Thou dost not go forth, O God, with our
     armies.
O grant us help against the foe,
for vain is the help of man!
With God we shall do valiantly;
it is he who will tread down our foes.

O God, thou hast rejected us, broken our defenses; thou hast been angry; oh, restore us. Thou hast made the land to quake; repair its breaches, because it is tottering. *Thou hast made thy people suffer hard things; thou hast given us wine to drink that made us reel.* [What a splendid expression for forgetfulness!] *Thou hast set up a banner for those who fear thee; that thy beloved may be delivered, give victory by thy right hand and answer us! Who will bring me to the fortified city? Hast thou not rejected us, O God?*

Thou dost not go forth, O God, with our armies. In
the daily battle, You no longer go forth with me; in
our house, You no longer go forth with us. *O grant
us help against the foe, for vain is the help of man!*
A miracle is not something we can do ourselves; a
miracle is the fruit of true asking. We cannot escape
from this: a cut has to occur, a split must take place,
something basic has to shatter, because true asking
includes all this. This break unfolds according to a
lesson in humility that God must teach us in order
to bring us back to the simple awareness of our total
dependence, which is the great wonder of His glory.

A prayer of the liturgy of Holy Mass says, "God
our Father and protector, without you nothing is
holy, nothing has value." [There is nothing definitive, nothing complete, nothing that is not partial,
nothing that does not lie.] "Guide us to everlasting
life [the truth of things] by helping us to use wisely
the blessings you have given to the world."[1] Sin lords
over our life if we have not arrived at the point where
change begins, where the miracle begins: true asking,
the expression of true desire.

"Guide us to everlasting life by helping us to use
wisely the blessings you have given to the world."
What is eternal life? Is it not the mystery of God? And

1. Opening Prayer for the Seventeenth Sunday of Ordinary Time.

has not the mystery of God been splendidly revealed in Christ? How far we are from what ought to be the content of our intellect and our love for reality! Eternal life is Christ!

How do we wisely use the blessings given to the world in our constant search for eternal life? "From the dawn I look for you, O God, that I may see your power and your glory."[2] By asking that God's power and God's glory (which has been revealed to us in Christ) may be visible to us.

We use the blessings of the world by asking that this Presence be made manifest. These blessings are everything, from breathing to the imagination, from our own body to our relationships with other people or things. And what is the Church, if not the gathering of people who use the blessings given to the world in the constant search for Christ? He is not distant; Christ is the Mystery who has been made into presence.

This is the definition of vocation, the task inherent in it, the dynamic that translates it into act.

---

2. See Psalm 63:2. Text and commentary on page 74.

19

LET ME DWELL IN THY TENT
Psalm 61

Hear my cry, O God,
listen to my prayer;
from the end of the earth I call to thee,
when my heart is faint.
Lead thou me to the rock that is higher than I;
for thou art my refuge,
a strong tower against the enemy.
Let me dwell in thy tent for ever!
Oh to be safe under the shelter of thy wings!
For thou, O God, hast heard my vows,
thou hast given me the heritage of those who
*   fear thy name.*
Prolong the life of the king;
may his years endure to all generations!
May he be enthroned for ever before God;
bid steadfast love and faithfulness watch over
*   him!*

So will I ever sing praises to thy name,
as I pay my vows day after day.

From the end of the earth I call to thee [from the end of my earth], *when my heart is faint. Lead thou me to the rock that is higher than I* [a point of safety].

Do we have this cry inside us? Someone can be well because he is certain of being God's for eternity, and someone else, faced with the same things, can not be well, does not feel this certainty, has a faint heart. In either case, *Let me dwell in thy tent for ever,* we belong to God forever. These are not words that change with one's mood; they come from our judgment and from the freedom that chooses to cling to the truth.

The Psalms often speak of persecutors, of insolent men who do not follow God's law, of people who wrongfully persecute us and banish us. Let us remind ourselves that this hostile reality spoken of in most of the Psalms refers to a historical reality, but the truth of these words is in all of us and resounds in something inside of us. In fact, *my heart is faint,* so *lead thou me to the rock that is higher than I.* The enemy before whom God will be *a strong tower* is inside of me; the enemy who terrifies us, against whom we pray that God preserves us, is inside of us. The problem lies inside of us.

20

THY STEADFAST LOVE
IS BETTER THAN LIFE
Psalm 63

O God, thou art my God, I seek thee,
my soul thirsts for thee;
my flesh faints for thee,
as in a dry and weary land
where no water is.
So I have looked upon thee in the sanctuary,
beholding thy power and thy glory.
Because thy steadfast love is better than life,
my lips will praise thee.
So I will bless thee as long as I live;
I will lift up my hands and call on thy name.
My soul is feasted as with marrow and fat,
and my mouth praises thee with joyful lips,
when I think of thee upon my bed,
and meditate on thee in the watches of the
        night;

for thou hast been my help,
and in the shadow of thy wings I sing for joy.
My soul clings to thee;
thy right hand upholds me. (Ps. 63:1–8)

O God, thou art my God, I seek thee, my soul thirsts for thee. Our day is a hunger and thirst for satisfaction and solidity, expressed by our flesh and blood: *my flesh faints for thee,* because without God I would be dry and weary, without water. We never have what we want, and so our flesh, the awareness of ourselves, faints for God, who is our origin and our end. This is why I am moved from my house. *I have looked upon thee in the sanctuary:* the sanctuary, or temple, or dwelling place of God is that place where everyone who recognizes that God is everything comes together. God is truly everything, not only because "apart from me you can do nothing" (John 15:5) — nothing! — but because "in Him all things hold together" (see 1 Cor. 8:6; Col. 1:17; Rev. 4:11).

So I have looked upon thee in the sanctuary, beholding thy power and thy glory. In the dwelling place of God, reality has already been looked upon, judged, and deliberately lived in the light of the great presence and in what that presence evokes. The grace, the steadfast love of God is God present in our life. Grace is Jesus.

Thy steadfast love is better than life, than anything that exists in life. *Thy steadfast love is better than life:* We must let this prayer become the habitual object of our thinking. At first it will be almost hazy, almost impenetrable, but if we repeat it, the truth in it will clarify its meaning.

I think of thee upon my bed, even when weighed down by the hardships of the day, *and meditate on thee in the watches of the night.* When I cannot sleep, I think of God. I do not think of Him abstractly, but concretely, because He is within my experience of the present. He is verifiable. He has, in fact, *been my help.* Whatever good there is in my life is because of His presence.

In the shadow of thy wings I sing for joy: So there is a joy quivering in my heart, because I am in God's arms. This is a perfect image of the relationship between God and man, as laid down by God and revealed by Jesus: *My soul clings to thee; thy right hand upholds me.*

It has always been easy to call ourselves back to this supreme image, notwithstanding the effects and nature of original sin, an image that is so charged with a creaturely tenderness, with purity, it has the freshness of the creative moment of the man and woman who walk along in love, step by step along the path they travel together. No other creatures in the universe are so united, so drawn to completion.

Jesus came to reestablish reality in the authenticity in which the hand of God and the breath of the Spirit created it.

God established the form of our relationship with Him; we did not choose it. Thanks be to God that Socrates did not choose it, that Aristotle did not think of it, that Hegel did not define it, nor even Pascal ... or any of the most religious of the philosophers. God Himself thought of it, and Jesus told it to us: our relationship with God has a familiarity without equal, in which each one of us is called to be part of the Mystery, part of God.

It is the way that "still living in the flesh, we live in the faith of the Son of God" (see Gal. 2:20). Our soul clings to Him, and His strength upholds us. He loved me and gave Himself for me: there is nothing simpler or anything greater that can be said.

My soul clings to thee; thy right hand upholds me: This renewing phrase literally consecrates the physicality of His presence, the vocational companionship. *My soul clings to thee; thy right hand upholds me,* because His right hand, the muscle of His right hand is the shared dwelling place to which my vocation has led me, and the physical reality of

His presence to which my soul clings is the companionship to which my vocation has led me. The
whole teaching lies here: it is how mercy, passion,
and yearning for the world are upheld and nourished.

If these words are true for us, *O God, thou art my
God, I seek thee, my soul thirsts for thee; my flesh
faints for thee, as in a dry and weary land where
no water is,* then we will not walk the road of life
like everyone else does. Because this road must be
an example (and I am thinking of the undertaking of
this road, which is to be an example for the other
roads), we cannot go forth on this road with our
head buried in the sand, without awareness of what
it means, foolish and slow to believe, as the Lord said
when He met the disciples on the way to Emmaus
(see Luke 24:25). We cannot walk this road without
saying: *So I will bless thee as long as I live; I will lift
up my hands and call on thy name. My soul is feasted
as with marrow and fat, and my mouth praises thee
with joyful lips.*

If these things are not sought every day, are not
the content of our heart and of our awareness, then
how can we manage to live, how can we manage to
walk? God's right hand, His name will be revealed
in the gladness of our faces.

Gladness cannot be born without certainty. This
is why it is the echo of faith. Gladness is born of

certainty. Saying that God exists, that destiny exists, that eternity exists, is of value only insofar as it signifies a genuine link, a connection, a relationship present now. Saying that the Lord exists means that I am the servant of the Lord, that I am created by the Lord. Saying that we have a destiny and that there is Paradise and eternity means that this moment has an eternal value and is the instrument of my happiness. Destiny determines the present. Certainty captures the present.

21

PRESERVE MY LIFE
FROM DREAD OF THE ENEMY
Psalm 64

Hear my voice, O God, in my complaint;
preserve my life from dread of the enemy,
hide me from the secret plots of the wicked,
from the scheming of evildoers,
who whet their tongues like swords,
who aim bitter words like arrows,
shooting from ambush at the blameless,
shooting at him suddenly
and without fear.
They hold fast to their evil purpose;
they talk of laying snares secretly,
thinking, "Who can see us?
Who can search out our crimes?
We have thought out a cunningly conceived
*   plot."*

> *For the inward mind and heart of a man are*
>   *deep!*
> *But God will shoot his arrow at them;*
> *they will be wounded suddenly.*
> *Because of their tongue he will bring them to*
>   *ruin;*
> *all who see them will wag their heads.*
> *Then all men will fear;*
> *they will tell what God has wrought,*
> *and ponder what he has done.*
> *Let the righteous rejoice in the* LORD,
> *and take refuge in him!*
> *Let all the upright in heart glory!*

Preserve my life from dread of the enemy, because the enemy's strength is the terror he instills in us. *Hide me from the secret plots of the wicked,* who are *shooting at* me *suddenly.* But the enemy, evil, is also in us; it holds fast and lays snares secretly, saying, "Who can see these snares?" Feeling outside our limits, beyond our own boundaries, like a stranger on the road where God has called us together — this is all a snare. We will be able to deny Him once we have turned away from Him in this way.

Let the righteous rejoice in the LORD, not because he has no enemies, not because he is crying out from the limits of his own "I," but because he places his hope in God.

The words of Jeremiah were providential: "Stand by the roads, and look, and ask for the ancient paths, where the good way is"! Ask when everything is dark or strange in the present. Ask for the ancient paths, where the good way is and take it, "and find rest for your souls" (Jer. 6:16).

22

Upon Thee I Have Leaned from My Birth
Psalm 71

In thee, O Lord, do I take refuge;
let me never be put to shame!
In thy righteousness deliver me and rescue me;
incline thy ear to me, and save me!
Be thou to me a rock of refuge,
a strong fortress, to save me,
for thou art my rock and my fortress.
Rescue me, O my God, from the hand of the
*   wicked,*
from the grasp of the unjust and cruel man.
For thou, O Lord, art my hope,
my trust, O Lord, from my youth.
Upon thee I have leaned from my birth;
thou art he who took me from my mother's
*   womb.*
My praise is continually of thee.

I have been as a portent to many;
but thou art my strong refuge.
My mouth is filled with thy praise,
and with thy glory all the day.
Do not cast me off in the time of old age;
forsake me not when my strength is spent.
O God, from my youth thou hast taught me,
and I still proclaim thy wondrous deeds.
So even to old age and gray hairs,
O God, do not forsake me,
till I proclaim thy might
to all generations to come. (Ps. 71:1–9, 17–18)

Rescue me, O God, from the hand of the wicked....
For thou, O Lord, art my hope, my trust, O LORD,
from my youth. Upon thee I have leaned from my
birth; thou art he who took me from my mother's
womb. My praise is continually of thee. This could
be the definition of life itself.

In prayer, the recapitulation of our own life flows
forth: my way of thinking, of feeling, of acting is so
unique that *I have been as a portent to many,* but
thou art my strong refuge. Do not cast me off in the
time of old age; forsake me not when my strength is
spent.

23

WHO CUTS OFF THE SPIRIT OF PRINCES

Psalm 76

But thou, terrible art thou!
Who can stand before thee
when once thy anger is roused?
From the heavens thou didst utter judgment;
the earth feared and was still,
when God arose to establish judgment
to save all the oppressed of the earth.
Surely the wrath of men shall praise thee;
the residue of wrath thou wilt gird upon thee.
Make your vows to the LORD your God, and
    perform them;
let all around him bring gifts
to him who is to be feared,
who cuts off the spirit of princes,
who is terrible to the kings of the earth.
               (Ps. 76:7–12)

"Grace is still more mysterious and more profound than beauty. Grace is still more arbitrary, more free, more sovereign, more perfectly illogical and gratu- itous; also disquieting, like everything that is given gratuitously. Power of grace, eternal power of the eternal blood, of an eternal blood, the blood of Jesus Christ."[1] When, Lord, will our souls share in the grace that you have given to the convert Charles Péguy?

"What is most unforeseen in Christianity," Péguy says elsewhere, "is always the event as something al- ways and everywhere. It is enough to have lived a little bit outside of history books to know, to have experienced that what we want most to see occur is generally what happens the least, and what we do not want to see occur is generally what happens."[2]

We do not yet know. We are not children, in the ethical sense. We are not *the oppressed of the earth*. The oppressed, the humble of the earth, are the ones who know. They know, because through being it has been revealed to them; and they have not re- nounced this original dependent position of being but accepted it. The more often the Presence is laid

---

1. Charles Péguy, *Devant les accidents de la gloire temporelle*, cited in T. Dejond, *Charles Péguy: L'espérance d'un salut universelle* (Namur: Culture et Vérité, 1989), 35–36.
2. Charles Péguy, *Pensées* (Paris: Gallimard, 1934), 45.

out for us, the greater the danger that we will not accept it, or qualify it with our "ifs," "ands," and "buts." We want, we set the measure of time; we set the method of responding to it.

24

RESTORE US, O GOD
Psalm 80

Give ear, O Shepherd of Israel,
thou who leadest Joseph like a flock!
Thou who art enthroned upon the cherubim,
    shine forth
before Ephraim and Benjamin and Manasseh!
Stir up thy might,
and come to save us!
Restore us, O God;
let thy face shine, that we may be saved!
O LORD God of hosts,
how long wilt thou be angry
with thy people's prayers?
Thou hast fed them with the bread of tears,
and given them tears to drink in full measure.
Thou dost make us the scorn of our neighbors;
and our enemies laugh among themselves.

> *Restore us, O God of hosts;*
> *let thy face shine, that we may be saved!*
>   (Ps. 80:1–7)

Restore us, O God.... Thou hast fed them with the bread of tears, and given them tears to drink in full measure. Thou dost make us the scorn of our neighbors; and our enemies laugh among themselves.

Our enemies are first of all inside us; they are the earthly reality that is held inside us. The enemy is also outside, but he is strong only if he takes root inside us. What can save us?

Restore us, O God of hosts; let thy face shine, that we may be saved!

God has let His face shine; it is the face of Christ.

25

BLESSED ARE THE MEN WHOSE STRENGTH IS IN THEE
Psalm 84

How lovely is thy dwelling place,
O LORD of hosts!
My soul longs, yea, faints
for the courts of the LORD;
my heart and flesh sing for joy
to the living God.
Even the sparrow finds a home,
and the swallow a nest for herself,
where she may lay her young,
at thy altars, O LORD of hosts,
my King and my God.
Blessed are those who dwell in thy house,
ever singing thy praise!
Blessed are the men whose strength is in thee,
in whose heart are the highways to Zion.
As they go through the valley of Baca

they make it a place of springs;
the early rain also
covers it with pools.
They go from strength to strength;
the God of gods will be seen in Zion.
O LORD God of hosts, hear my prayer;
give ear, O God of Jacob!
Behold our shield, O God;
look upon the face of thine anointed!
For a day in thy courts is better
than a thousand elsewhere.
I would rather be a doorkeeper in the house of
*   my God*
than dwell in the tents of wickedness.
For the LORD God is a sun and shield;
he bestows favor and honor.
No good thing does the LORD withhold
from those who walk uprightly.
O LORD of hosts,
blessed is the man who trusts in thee!

Are we able to say, when we think of our companionship, of our house, of the people that we form, "My soul faints for all this; my heart and my flesh sing for joy in this present sign of God, in this living presence of Christ"?

Blessed are those who dwell in thy house, ever singing thy praise! Blessed are the men whose strength is in thee, in whose heart are the highways to Zion. Man finds his strength in the living God and goes *from strength to strength.* This is the certainty that awaits those who are about to enter this companionship in a committed way.[1] If they see around them a contrary sign, it can be conquered by the mercy of God.

Look upon the face of thine anointed. There is an unmistakable sign of the truth of our path, its radiant "morning star": gladness of heart (see Rev. 2:28; 22:16). If our heart is shot through with sorrow for our own evil, our own sin, and our own failings, even so gladness of heart will be nourished by love for Christ.

It is not necessary to live a life dedicated to Christ without gladness. The Lord has His gift ready for each one of us: the radiant morning star, which lasts all day long, which lasts all our life: His gladness. "These things I have spoken to you, that my joy may be in you, and that your joy may be full" (John 15:11).

---

1. Father Giussani is referring here to the moment of "profession" which ratifies the definitive admission into the Aspirants of the Association *Memores Domini*. —Trans.

26

THOU WAST FAVORABLE TO THY LAND
Psalm 85

LORD, *thou wast favorable to thy land;*
thou didst restore the fortunes of Jacob.
Thou didst forgive the iniquity of thy people;
thou didst pardon all their sin.
Thou didst withdraw all thy wrath;
thou didst turn from thy hot anger.
Restore us again, O God of our salvation,
and put away thy indignation toward us!
Wilt thou be angry with us for ever?
Wilt thou prolong thy anger to all generations?
Wilt thou not revive us again,
that thy people may rejoice in thee?
Show us thy steadfast love, O LORD,
and grant us thy salvation.
Let me hear what God the LORD *will speak,*
for he will speak peace

to his people, to his saints,
to those who turn to him in their hearts.
Surely his salvation is at hand for those who
        fear him,
that glory may dwell in our land.
Steadfast love and faithfulness will meet;
righteousness and peace will kiss each other.
Faithfulness will spring up from the ground,
and righteousness will look down from the sky.
Yea, the LORD will give what is good,
and our land will yield its increase.
Righteousness will go before him,
and make his footsteps a way.

LORD, *thou wast favorable to thy land; thou didst
restore the fortunes of Jacob.* We are God's land, because with us, as it is written, "Having loved his own
who were in the world, he loved them to the end"
(John 13:1). God has deepened the covenant to the
very wellspring of our thought, our emotions, and
our freedom, giving us a great image, idea, and feeling of Him, and a great will for Him. On a human
level we cannot think of anything greater, because
this thing is virginity. It is what the covenant of Christ
is for man; He is all in all (Col. 3:11).

We are His land. How often He brought us back
from exile, from the lie that exploited our weakness,

our laziness, slackness, small-mindedness, opposition! How often He brought us back from the exile imposed by the lie that used our restlessness, our presumption, or our taste for power against us! The principle of evil imposed this exile in us, but we were the sons of Jacob, God's land. How often He has brought back *the fortunes of Jacob!*

Thou didst forgive the iniquity of thy people; thou didst pardon all their sin. Wilt thou be angry with us for ever? Wilt thou prolong thy anger to all generations? Wilt thou not revive us again, that thy people may rejoice in thee? Show us thy steadfast love, O LORD, *and grant us thy salvation. Let me hear what God the* LORD *will speak, for he will speak of peace.*

The Lord came for the man who knows he is weak, for the man who recognizes his frailty and desires a strength that is not his, who desires the power of salvation that belongs to God. The Pharisees and scribes were more wretched than the rest, but Christ did not come for them, because they believed they were good as they were.

The Lord did not die so that His cross would fall down on us as a judgment to destroy us, but so that it would grant mercy, to renew us in contrition and in gladness, in the mortification of ourselves and in the cheerfulness of self-abandonment.

Psalm 85 says, *His salvation is at hand for those who fear him.* To fear the Lord means to live the knowledge of His lordship: "You are the Lord, my God, my all."

Glory may dwell in our land. Steadfast love and faithfulness will meet. Faithfulness will spring up from the ground, and righteousness will look down from the sky. Yea, the LORD will give what is good, and our land will yield its increase. The Lord will give His good; then our land will yield its increase. The Lord will give Christ, His Son. This good that is Christ shows itself in the history that the Father has written for each of us. The good which is Christ shows itself in the grace that is bound to life's occasions. The season of Advent is grace, as the beginning of a new year is grace. But how completely this good takes on the value of grace is revealed when suffering, the cross, death, touches our life. The Lord wants our land to bear its fruit; if He has given us this good of the cross, it means that time has come when our land may bear its fruit. We must stand up straight, lift ourselves out of our tired, distracted position, like the flower that is the beginning of the fruit and the pledge of this profound promise.

27

HOW GREAT ARE THY WORKS
Psalm 92

It is good to give thanks to the LORD,
to sing praises to thy name, O Most High;
to declare thy steadfast love in the morning,
and thy faithfulness by night,
to the music of the lute and the harp,
to the melody of the lyre.
For thou, O LORD, hast made me glad by thy
*   work;*
at the works of thy hands I sing for joy.
How great are thy works, O LORD!
Thy thoughts are very deep!
The dull man cannot know,
the stupid cannot understand this:
that, though the wicked sprout like grass
and all evildoers flourish,
but thou, O LORD, art on high for ever.

For lo, thy enemies, O LORD,
for lo, thy enemies shall perish;
all evildoers shall be scattered.
But thou hast exalted my horn like that of the
      wild ox;
thou hast poured over me fresh oil.
My eyes have seen the downfall of my enemies,
my ears have heard the doom of my evil
      assailants.
The righteous flourish like the palm tree,
and grow like a cedar in Lebanon.
They are planted in the house of the LORD,
they flourish in the courts of our God.
They still bring forth fruit in old age,
they are ever full of sap and green,
to show that the LORD is upright;
he is my rock, and there is no unrighteousness
      in him.
they are doomed to destruction for ever.

In the morning we declare God's steadfast love, God's truth in the deep night. God has entered and dwells in human flesh. He has entered the experience of man, so that it is no longer human experience if it is not conscious of this and does not follow this factor, if this factor does not act upon it.

For thou, O LORD, hast made me glad by thy work; at the works of thy hands I sing for joy. The work of thy hands is God's presence in our experience, in our existence.

The dull man cannot know. The man who is without sense, who cannot give meaning to what he is and what he does, cannot know, does not tend towards God, does not open himself up to God.

But thou hast exalted my horn like that of the wild ox; thou hast poured over me fresh oil. The first rule of prayer is weighing the words you say so that they become your own. There is nothing that reduces a person more than prayer said with formality, because it is a lie, not a calculated one, but a lie nevertheless. It is dressing up, like when you were a child, dressing up in clothes of something great. Most people — if they go to church — do not weigh the words they say. If this is unbearably sad for someone who has this feeling for prayer, how it must be for God, for Christ, when He says to the prophet, "Their lips speak to me, but their heart is very distant" (see Isa. 29:13).

Think of something that interested you and that you did because it interested you. What you put into that, that is the will, because if you care about something, you put all the energy of devotion into what you recognize as true.

They still bring forth fruit in old age, they are ever full of sap and green, to show that the LORD *is upright.*

If we were to simply let our life go on, it would roll toward fossilization as spirit and meaning. Our life would perhaps be externally involved, laden with work, outside the home or even within the home. Perhaps it would even be so intense that everyone would notice it. Yet as authentic life, as meaning and as spirit, it would keep on withdrawing. If on the other hand, we could project into the future the heart that we are living with now, the passage of the Psalm would be realized: *They are ever full of sap and green, to show that the* LORD *is upright.*

Try to oppose another goal of life on this affirmation of Scripture!

Imposing anything on this intention erases the greatest possible human joy — namely, *Ecce quam bonum et quam iucundum habitare fratres in unum,* "Behold, how good and pleasant it is when brothers dwell in unity!" (Ps. 133:1). This joy is obliterated because our lives, then, are not determined by the continual newness that sets us in the eternal. The content of our life, of our personality is separated and fragmented by goals that, whirling about, try to superimpose themselves on the one goal that gives peace to the heart, intensity to time, and that obliterates the restlessness that, like a cancer, alters the tissues of our life.

How great are thy works, O LORD! Thy thoughts are very deep! The dull man cannot know. This confession lies at the foundation of every day of Lent, when we pay attention to it in the way that we should throughout the year.

The dull man cannot know, the stupid cannot understand this. But if we *wicked sprout like grass,* there awaits for us *destruction for ever:* the eternal destruction of everything we do, which will be like the crumbling of a damp and rotten wall, or like wormy fruit that cannot be offered without shame.

But thou, O LORD, art on high for ever: God wins; He penetrates our distractions and weaknesses. His strength is greater than our wretchedness. This is the stream of gladness that Lent brings forth. Whoever wants to be God's enemy will perish; and everything that he does in life, as he will see as the years go by, is meaningless.

But *thou,* who are stronger than my wretchedness, *hast exalted my horn like that of the wild ox; my eyes have seen the downfall* of what I have done every day, of what I do and will do. Against *my evil assailants,* against all the distracting or evil suggestions that time hands to me at every moment, something in me will *flourish like the palm tree, and grow like a cedar in*

Lebanon. All the corners of my house will flourish — or rather, of God's house, because it is His gift. I recognize it as God's possession. God brings light, and makes straight a path through all the torture of our wretchedness.

Time will always bring forth fruit; time will make me full of sap and green.

The purpose of God giving you existence and of His possession of you will appear as the horizon of your life: *to show that the* LORD *is upright; he is my rock* in whom *there is no unrighteousness.*

28

THOU HAST DELIVERED
MY SOUL FROM DEATH
Psalm 116

*I love the LORD, because he has heard
my voice and my supplications.
Because he inclined his ear to me,
therefore I will call on him as long as I live.
The snares of death encompassed me;
the pangs of Sheol laid hold on me;
I suffered distress and anguish.
Then I called on the name of the LORD:
"O LORD, I beseech thee, save my life!"
Gracious is the LORD, and righteous;
our God is merciful.
The LORD preserves the simple;
when I was brought low, he saved me.
Return, O my soul, to your rest;
for the LORD has dealt bountifully with you.*

> *For thou hast delivered my*
> *soul from death,*
> *my eyes from tears,*
> *my feet from stumbling;*
> *I will walk before the* LORD
> *in the land of the living.*
>   (Ps. 116:1–9)

I love the LORD, *because he has heard my voice and my supplications.*

Did you wake up crying this morning? If so, you can still say, "*I love the* LORD," even if your life is wretched.

Your tears point to your will for existence. I love the Lord because He has compassion on me. From the depth of my cry arises the whole crescendo, ending with *I will walk before the* LORD.

I love the LORD, *because he has heard my voice and my supplications. Because he inclined his ear to me, therefore I will call on him as long as I live. The snares of death encompassed me; the pangs of Sheol laid hold on me; I suffered distress and anguish. Then I called on the name of the* LORD: *"O* LORD, *I beseech thee, save my life!" Gracious is the* LORD, *and righteous; our God is merciful. The* LORD *preserves the simple; when I was brought low, he saved me. Return, O my soul, to your rest; for the* LORD *has dealt bountifully with you. For thou hast delivered my soul from death, my eyes from tears, my feet from stumbling; I will walk before the* LORD *in the land of the living.*

The Mystery is righteous and merciful if we are humble and recognize that all comes from the Mystery.

When I was brought low, he saved me. Sadness and anguish, which try to oppress us, can be turned into an invocation: *"O* LORD, *I beseech thee, save my life!"* Thus the Lord *preserves the simple* and my soul returns to its rest, because the Lord delivers us from degradation and corruption. He lets us dry our tears.

29

I KEPT MY FAITH, EVEN WHEN I SAID, "I AM GREATLY AFFLICTED"
Psalm 116

I kept my faith, even when I said,
"I am greatly afflicted."
I said in my consternation,
"Men are all a vain hope."
What shall I render to the LORD
for all his bounty to me?
I will lift up the cup of salvation
and call on the name of the LORD,
I will pay my vows to the LORD
in the presence of all his people.
Precious in the sight of the LORD
is the death of his saints.
O LORD, I am thy servant,
I am thy servant, the son of thy handmaid.

Thou hast loosed my bonds.
I will offer to thee the sacrifice of thanksgiving
and call on the name of the LORD.
I will pay my vows to the LORD
in the presence of all his people,
in the courts of the house of the LORD,
in your midst, O Jerusalem.
Praise the LORD! (Ps. 116:10–19)

I kept my faith, even when I said, "I am greatly af-flicted." Precious in the sight of the LORD *is the death of his saints.*

Here is the principle and the explanation that sums up everything: *I kept my faith, even when I said, "I am greatly afflicted."* Even when I was in Mesopo-tamia, in Babylon, in exile, in desolation. *Precious in the sight of the* LORD *is the death of his saints.* Sorrow and sacrifice, whatever its nature, is precious in the eyes of the Lord; it is an instrument for our maturity and recognition of Him.

All of life is a story in which this principle is ap-parent. It is like a seed in the story of time. The story of time is created by God through conditions and influences: He allows you to knock your head or cause a disaster; He lets you have a headache or a stomachache; He leaves you to find yourself confused or alone.

Thou hast loosed my bonds and thus *I will pay my vows to the* LORD.

Thou hast loosed my bonds: the things that bind us are very concrete: any moment of our life, any of our expressions, any action; in each of them something must be loosed. None of these are abstract: life here and now is tomorrow morning when you get up or when you don't get up because you're sick; it's your work when it's going well and when it's not going well; it's when you're whimpering or when you're laughing too much.

Thou hast loosed my bonds; I will pay my vows to the LORD *in the presence of all his people. I kept my faith, even when I said, "I am greatly afflicted."* If the bond is loosed, if man is contrite, the vows to the Lord are paid in the presence of His people in the form of vocation. Vocation is our role in the life of the Church and of the world.

In your midst, O Jerusalem: This payment of vows to the Lord, in your midst, O Jerusalem, is what you do every day, as you eat, drink, enter into relationship, work, teach, run here and there (whether you need to or not), go to bed at a certain hour or keep silence: these are the concrete terms of our life, all our days: relationships, places, things to do.

I kept my faith even when I said, "I am greatly afflicted." Precious in the sight of the LORD *is the death of his saints,* even the death of the one who says, "I no longer see anything," because it is through this nakedness that God is affirmed. When someone is in this condition, the bond is loosed; this man is faithful to the circumstances in which God has placed us.

30

The Faithfulness of the Lord Endures for Ever
Psalm 117

Praise the LORD, all nations!
Extol him, all peoples!
For great is his steadfast love toward us;
and the faithfulness of the LORD endures for
  ever.
Praise the LORD!

Uncertainty most undermines our awareness of belonging to Christ, or causes doubt that Christ can overcome our disgraced humanity.

If our awareness of belonging is to develop and be alive in us, the sentiment needed in the life of the Christian, the victory that overcomes the world, is faith.

Great is his steadfast love toward us, and the faithfulness of the LORD endures for ever.

God's faithfulness means He chose us and formed a covenant with us. Certainty of this allows us to understand that we belong to our Lord.

3 1

The Lord Is My Strength and My Song
Psalm 118

O give thanks to the Lord, for he is good;
his steadfast love endures for ever!
Let Israel say,
"His steadfast love endures for ever."
Let the house of Aaron say,
"His steadfast love endures for ever."
Let those who fear the Lord say,
"His steadfast love endures for ever."
Out of my distress I called on the Lord;
the Lord answered me and set me free.
With the Lord on my side I do not fear.
What can man do to me?
The Lord is on my side to help me;
I shall look in triumph on those who hate me.
It is better to take refuge in the Lord
than to put confidence in man.

It is better to take refuge in the LORD
than to put confidence in princes.
All nations surrounded me;
in the name of the LORD I cut them off!
They surrounded me, surrounded me on every
     side;
in the name of the LORD I cut them off!
They surrounded me like bees,
they blazed like a fire of thorns;
in the name of the LORD I cut them off!
I was pushed hard, so that I was falling,
but the LORD helped me.
The LORD is my strength and my song;
he has become my salvation.
Hark, glad songs of victory
in the tents of the righteous:
"The right hand of the LORD does valiantly,
the right hand of the LORD is exalted,
the right hand of the LORD does valiantly!"
I shall not die, but I shall live,
and recount the deeds of the LORD.
The LORD has chastened me sorely,
but he has not given me over to death.
                                        (Ps. 118:1–18)

What can man do to me? The man who is in me,
the man who is in you, what can he do to you? The

Lord is with you, so do not be afraid. The man within can make you err and err again; but love has washed sin away. Love washes away sin a hundred thousand times a day.

The true drama is faith, the victory that conquers the flesh (see 1 John 5:4). "Strengthen our weak faith [in all of us faith is weak], showing the glorious wounds [it cannot take anything away anymore]."[1]

In a letter to his wife, Emmanuel Mounier wrote about their little girl, who had become mentally handicapped, "The world is made up of beggars, who are begging for the certainty of our love, from us to whom it has been given. We are the few, the rich in this world, rich in Christ, that is, in God, in God made flesh."[2]

What makes the work that our vocation dictates so improbable? What makes it so difficult?

There is only one comfort, in the true sense of the word — a strength that does not come from us but that is in us through the presence of someone Other. Whoever we are, *his steadfast love endures for ever.*

---

1. Verse from a hymn for Morning Prayer of Ordinary Time, "The Dawn Shines Forth with Light." See text and commentary in Luigi Giussani, *Tutta la terra desidera il Tuo volto* (Cinisello Balsalmo: Edizioni San Paolo, 2000), 30–33.

2. See Emmanuel Mounier, *Lettere sul dolore* (Milan: BUR, 1995), 61.

He has chosen us; He impacts our life and draws it into goodness, making it an instrument of the building of His kingdom.

Those who hate me are those who make us sad and distracted. *Those who hate me* are those who distance us from others. The one who hates you, the enemy, is the one who judges your life by what you do in the world, or by what you don't have.

But surrounded by enemies who hide inside of us and find collaboration in everything outside of us, we cannot be passive. We can be nothing but active and do our "work." We share in the life of God who is "the eternal worker," as Christ calls Him (see John 5:17). We share in His eternal work in our struggle against falsehood and the evil that is in us and around us: this is our life's work. *It is better to take refuge in the LORD than to put confidence in man.*

The LORD is my strength and my song: This is what the poor man says, the one who has nothing. Is it true for us, this *give thanks to the LORD, for he is good*? Do we experience that *his steadfast love endures for ever*?

He has become my salvation. Hark, glad songs of victory in the tents of the righteous, in the thick of the feelings of my existence, in the thick of the feelings of myself. *I shall not die, but I shall live, and recount the deeds of the LORD:* This is the work that the mystery of Easter must realize in us very urgently, the recovery, the renewal of the authenticity of our faith.

Each of us must ask that the paschal mystery of Christ more deeply penetrate the flesh and bones of our person in our everyday life, and that we can use our works as its sign.

There are *glad songs of victory* because *his steadfast love endures for ever:* What wonder that we find ourselves again in the presence of Christ, now that, shaking ourselves out of distraction, we are compelled to look Him in the face, see His real presence in the mystery of the Eucharist. How joyous it is to rediscover that His presence arises, undisturbed by our lives and our betrayals, the gravest of which is our forgetfulness. We feel this presence of His penetrating us.

The affirmation of His lordship continues in us despite our wickedness and small-mindedness. *I shall not die, but I shall live, and recount the deeds of the* LORD. This is the theme that each one of us must repeat as a test of the capacity of our heart for renewal.

I shall not die, but I shall live, and recount the deeds of the LORD, awestruck, amazed, contemplating His endless mercy.

32

I Will Fix My Eyes
on Thy Ways
Psalm 119

How can a young man keep his way pure?
By guarding it according to thy word.
With my whole heart I seek thee;
let me not wander from thy commandments!
I have laid up thy word in my heart,
that I might not sin against thee.
Blessed be thou, O Lord;
teach me thy statutes!
With my lips I declare
all the ordinances of thy mouth.
In the way of thy testimonies I delight
as much as in all riches.
I will meditate on thy precepts,
and fix my eyes on thy ways.
I will delight in thy statutes;
I will not forget thy word. (Ps. 119:9–16)

In the way of thy testimonies I delight as much as in all riches.

The glory of Christ's resurrection begins here: in the relationships among us, among men made different. Relationships among people, between man and woman, among people who live together as among strangers, the relationship with things, the toll we pay for being able to eat, for our work, which expresses the passion for creativity, the relationship with the past, the present, the future, the relationship with our errors: everything must be transfigured in the glory of the resurrection, like a humble piece of blank paper onto which the genius of man casts shape and color.

33

IN THY RIGHTEOUSNESS
GIVE ME LIFE
Psalm 119

Teach me, O LORD, the way of thy statutes;
and I will keep it to the end.
Give me understanding, that I may keep thy
     law
and observe it with my whole heart.
Lead me in the path of thy commandments,
for I delight in it.
Incline my heart to thy testimonies,
and not to gain!
Turn my eyes from looking at vanities;
and give me life in thy ways.
Confirm to thy servant thy promise,
which is for those who fear thee.
Turn away the reproach which I dread;
for thy ordinances are good.

> *Behold, I long for thy precepts;*
> *in thy righteousness give me life!*
> (Ps. 119:33–40)

Teach me, Lord, Your way: The entire theoretical discourse — on the appeal to the principles of love for one's neighbor, spending time and energy on the needs of the other, and giving God His time — is inherent in this directive. *Teach me, O LORD, the way of thy statutes:* Not a form, but a life, a life that creates a form; indeed, the more the law is a life, the more it generates the full form of human intensity and gladness, of usefulness for others and for oneself.

Turn my eyes from looking at vanities; and give me life in thy ways.

Turn my eyes from looking at vanities, at the ephemeral aspect of things, which is deceptive. If we say that we want something that we like because then we would be happy, it is a lie, because we won't be!

Give me life in thy ways, make me ever more faithful to things as You have made them, to things pursued and used according to the design with which You have made them.

Turn my gaze from falsehood and illusion. Our prayers are meant to limit the deception of life and augment obedience to the plan of God in our life. They lead us toward gladness in our life. The correctness of our way of following will show in our greater gladness.

What You have done in my life is for my good, because You are just (God is faithful to Himself) and You restore my life. *Confirm to thy servant thy promise, which is for those who fear thee. Turn away the reproach which I dread; for thy ordinances are good.*

God keeps his promises to His servant; the promise is made to those who respect Him. He takes away the dishonor that so saddens us, for His decrees are kind.

In thy righteousness give me life.

Righteousness, or justice, is the plan by which God made and guides the world. There exists no other acceptable meaning of justice. It is Christ, because Christ is the plan of God in the world.

In thy righteousness give me life: Let me live in God's Word, in the plan He has made for me.

34

LET THY STEADFAST LOVE COME TO ME
Psalm 119

Let thy steadfast love come to me, O LORD,
thy salvation according to thy promise;
then I shall have an answer for those who taunt
*   me,*
for I trust in thy word.
And take not the word of truth utterly out of
*   my mouth,*
for my hope is in thy ordinances.
I will keep thy law continually,
for ever and ever;
and I shall walk at liberty,
for I have sought thy precepts.
I will also speak of thy testimonies before kings,
and shall not be put to shame;
for I find my delight in thy commandments,
which I love.

I revere thy commandments, which I love,
and I will meditate on thy statutes.
                                        (Ps. 119:41–48)

And take not the word of truth utterly out of my mouth. We must never do anything out of habit. Habit confounds reason. If we say prayer out of habit, we are fooling with Almighty God.

We must overcome our tendency toward habit in the things we do to impose humanity on the mechanism of habit. We need to give meaning to what we do, even if we do it a thousand times. We must be aware of and love what we have in front of us. Otherwise we will confuse novelty with change, and they are not the same.

We read in Psalm 119, *Let thy steadfast love come to me, O LORD.* Think of nothingness as a great sea of darkness; out of this nothingness comes forth the starry sky. Steadfast love, or grace, is the darkness of our mind and of our heart lit up with stars, with the words and deeds of God, and with His creatures, each of which is a work of art.

Let thy steadfast love come to me, O LORD: that I may understand. Salvation is the affirmation of everything that is, the valuing of everything.

35

REMEMBER THY WORD
Psalm 119

Remember thy word to thy servant,
in which thou hast made me hope.
This is my comfort in my affliction
that thy promise gives me life.
Godless men utterly deride me,
but I do not turn away from thy law.
When I think of thy ordinances from of old,
I take comfort, O LORD.
Hot indignation seizes me because of the
        wicked,
who forsake thy law.
Thy statutes have been my songs
in the house of my pilgrimage.
I remember thy name in the night, O LORD,
and keep thy law.
This blessing has fallen to me,
that I have kept thy precepts. (Ps. 119:49–56)

Thy statutes have been my songs in the house of my pilgrimage.

The Letter to the Hebrews speaks of the Patriarchs who lived in the Promised Land, but they had another, more permanent city (see Heb. 11:9–10). This is the feeling with which we must live in our homes, work, society, everywhere.

Remember thy word in which thou hast made me hope.

Hope is certainty about the future. Certainty is founded on something that has already happened; it rests on something present.

The reason for this hope for Israel is that God has freed them, and if He has freed them, it is in order to carry them to the very end. Hope is the certainty that God has freed me. There exists nothing more joyful, nothing more intensely human in life than to know this.

Outside of the influence of the Spirit, a person cannot comprehend the experience of devotion that binds the faithful to authority, that is, to the point where God touches, calls, and guides our life, that devotion that affirms itself in the cross of the mortified exuberance of one's own genius or of one's own plan of life.

36

LET THY STEADFAST LOVE
BE READY TO COMFORT ME
Psalm 119

Thy hands have made and fashioned me;
give me understanding that I may learn thy
*   commandments.*
Those who fear thee shall see me and rejoice,
because I have hoped in thy word.
I know, O LORD, that thy judgments are right,
and that in faithfulness thou hast afflicted me.
Let thy steadfast love be ready to comfort me
according to thy promise to thy servant.
Let thy mercy come to me, that I may live;
for thy law is my delight.
Let the godless be put to shame,
because they have subverted me with guile;
as for me, I will meditate on thy precepts.
Let those who fear thee turn to me,
that they may know thy testimonies.

> *May my heart be blameless in thy statutes,*
> *that I may not be put to shame!* (Ps. 119:73–80)

Those who fear thee shall see me and rejoice, because I have hoped in thy word.

I shall be a cause of joy for Your faithful ones, O Lord, because I have placed my hope in Your promises. *I know, O LORD, that thy judgments are right, and that in faithfulness thou hast afflicted me. Let thy steadfast love be ready to comfort me according to thy promise to thy servant. Let thy mercy come to me, that I may live; for thy law is my delight.*

Let Your mercy now console me, as You have promised to those who are faithful to You. Let Your kindness come back to me and I will feel reborn, because You are the wellspring of my calm and of my song.

There is only one answer, and it has been introduced to us by the passage of the Gospel that comes at the beginning of Lent — the beginning of God's judgment on our life. When the demon tempts Jesus with worldly value, born of the flesh, of the blood, of the life of society, of power, Jesus answers, "No." Because "it is written, 'Man shall not live by bread alone, but by every word that proceeds from the mouth of God'" (Matt. 4:4). The word of God is the new and eternal covenant.

The Psalm proceeds coherently: "In thy steadfast love spare my life, that I may keep the testimonies of thy mouth."[1] If God preserves my life, I will keep His laws; I will obey Him.

---

1. Psalm 119:88. See text and commentary, page 129.

37

IN THY STEADFAST LOVE
SPARE MY LIFE
Psalm 119

My soul languishes for thy salvation;
I hope in thy word.
My eyes fail with watching for thy promise;
I ask, "When wilt thou comfort me?"
For I have become like a wineskin in the
*   smoke,*
yet I have not forgotten thy statutes.
How long must thy servant endure?
When wilt thou judge those who persecute me?
Godless men have dug pitfalls for me,
men who do not conform to thy law.
All thy commandments are sure;
they persecute me with falsehood; help me!
They have almost made an end of me on
*   earth;*
but I have not forsaken thy precepts.

In thy steadfast love spare my life,
that I may keep the testimonies of thy mouth.
                                    (Ps. 119:81–88)

My soul languishes for thy salvation because *I hope in thy word.* God's words are for us; He puts them on the lips of our heart.

"Heaven and earth will pass away, but my words will not pass away" (Matt. 24:35; Mark 13:31; Luke 21:33). The word that He has said to our life will never pass away. Our path is the story of God in us, not the story of our feelings about God. Our path is the feeling that God has for me, not the feeling that I have for Him.

Those who persecute are not so much those outside of ourselves, as those we have inside us. Those on the outside are more evident and less harmful than those which are not evident, which Satan, the enemy, who hates man, uses inside us. Everything that does not follow His law is inside us.

Even were we to feel banished from the earth, from our land, from our very selves, we can say, *I have not forsaken thy precepts. In thy steadfast love spare my life.* How will the Lord ignore His chosen ones who cry out to Him day and night (see Luke 18:7)?

This cry, this begging for Christ, comes from the awareness of belonging, at play in every instant.

When wilt thou comfort me? We ask in the full certainty of peace, a calm asking.

For I have become like a wineskin in the smoke [dry and empty], *yet I have not forgotten thy statutes. ... All thy commandments are sure.* It is this faith that cries out, *When wilt thou comfort me?* and *In thy steadfast love spare my life.* Asking is salvation already present in us.

38

THY TESTIMONIES
ARE WONDERFUL
Psalm 119

Thy word is a lamp to my feet
and a light to my path.
I have sworn an oath and confirmed it,
to observe thy righteous ordinances.
I am sorely afflicted;
give me life, O LORD, according to thy word!
Accept my offerings of praise, O LORD,
and teach me thy ordinances.
Thy testimonies are wonderful;
therefore my soul keeps them.
The unfolding of thy word gives light;
it imparts understanding to the simple.
With open mouth I pant,
because I long for thy commandments.
Turn to me and be gracious to me,
as is thy wont toward those who love thy name.

Keep steady my steps according to thy promise,
and let no iniquity get dominion over me.
Redeem me from man's oppression,
that I may keep thy precepts.
Make thy face shine upon thy servant,
and teach me thy statutes.
My eyes shed streams of tears,
because men do not keep thy law.
Righteous art thou, O LORD,
and right are thy judgments.
Thou hast appointed thy testimonies in
  righteousness
and in all faithfulness.
My zeal consumes me,
because my foes forget thy words.
Thy promise is well tried,
and thy servant loves it.
I am small and despised,
yet I do not forget thy precepts.
Thy righteousness is righteous for ever,
and thy law is true.
Trouble and anguish have come upon me,
but thy commandments are my delight.
Thy testimonies are righteous for ever;
give me understanding that I may live.
                    (Ps. 119:105–8; 129–44)

A light to my path is thy word. Thy testimonies are wonderful; therefore my soul keeps them. His testimonies, His covenant is an event, historical and in our life.

The unfolding of thy word gives light; it imparts understanding to the simple. With open mouth I pant, because I long for thy commandments. Turn to me and be gracious to me, as is thy wont toward those who love thy name.... Thy testimonies are righteous for ever; give me understanding that I may live.

The event of the covenant is documented and manifested in communal gestures; its acme, the authentication of its expression in communal gestures, is expressed in the account of Nehemiah: "The assembly, both men and women and all who could hear with understanding, [was present].... And [he] opened the book in the sight of all the people" and "all the people wept when they heard the words of the law. Then [Nehemiah] said to them, 'Go your way, eat the fat and drink sweet wine and send portions to him for whom nothing is prepared; for this day is holy to our Lord; and do not be grieved, for the joy of the LORD is your strength'" (Neh. 8:2, 5, 9–10).

If we consider this very long psalm in its entirety (also known as the psalm of the law), the main point is that it prophesies the new law, which is the Spirit. The law reveals what God is for man; thus it is the Spirit who reveals what Christ is for man: "He shall reveal all things to you" (see John 15:26; 16:13–15).

The law reveals what God is for man because it underlines that man belongs to God. "I am the LORD your God" (Exod. 20:2): this is the beginning of the law.

We belong to God to be ourselves, because "I free you," says God. "You belong to me because I have freed you from Egypt" (Exod. 20:2). We belong to God because without Him we are nothing, without Him we perish. The Spirit is the Spirit of freedom, which is the Spirit of truth.

The law says that man belongs to God. Whoever does not have the Spirit of Christ is not His: he "does not belong to him" (Rom. 8:9), says Saint Paul. The Spirit is the wellspring of a moral impetus: "Let us walk according to the Spirit" (see Rom. 8:4; Gal. 5:25).

The form of the text is extremely important because it teaches us how to pray. To learn how to pray, we need to repeat incessantly. This Psalm repeats the same concept, as we repeat something we care about. If someone loves, he keeps on saying, "My love," "My treasure." And so our attention is called to what God is for man: law, because He is our liberator. God is law because man is "established" through Him. Man is not himself if he does not live the Spirit and the law.

The insistence on the proper object of our attention, that is, the law and the "way" (see Ps. 119:9, 27, 30–33, 101, 104, 128), show us that the law is a way to be ourselves. It is not a line of argument, but is evidence that we are "made by God," that we have been freed from the slavery of nothingness.

To observe the commandments means to repeat them continuously. One learns not by reasoning, but by continually repeating a truth, because what is truth must be repeatedly looked at in the face. We must struggle against forgetfulness.

Man's strength is the judgment of value. Love as esteem implies our struggle against the world's judgment of value. The world's judgment is reactive and instinctive; it is given when there is a blaze of affection or when one loves what is comfortable, pleasure. We need to struggle against whatever in us esteems something other than the law.

Hebrew is very concrete: *give me life* means, "Give me the energy to live now." *Redeem me* means, "Save me from the hostility of the world, from the world that attracts me." It means not only, "Save me," but also, "Teach me that You save me": that is, it takes account of the fragility and sadness that is in man, who does not even believe that he is saved. Even the understanding that He saves me has to come to me from Him.

The nature of the law is freedom; it is walking toward one's own wholeness, toward one's own fulfillment. It is not automatic; it is work, and it is what Almighty God expects each day of our intelligence, of our affection, of our will, of our capacity for sacrifice, of our love for the law, the path toward one's own destiny.

39

HE WHO KEEPS YOU WILL NOT SLUMBER
Psalm 121

I lift up my eyes to the hills.
From whence does my help come?
My help comes from the LORD,
who made heaven and earth.
He will not let your foot be moved,
he who keeps you will not slumber.
Behold, he who keeps Israel
will neither slumber nor sleep.
The LORD is your keeper;
the LORD is your shade
on your right hand.
The sun shall not smite you by day,
nor the moon by night.
The LORD will keep you from all evil;
he will keep your life.

> *The* LORD *will keep your going out and your*
>   *coming in*
> *from this time forth and for evermore.*

How can we, who are small, lost, unsure, weak, and contradictory, be His witnesses, since He has looked upon us for this purpose?

God does not create a being for no reason. He already has you in His sight. Salvation is near to us, says Psalm 121: *My help comes from the* LORD, *who made heaven and earth. He will not let your foot be moved.* He will steady your foot, He will make it firm on the rock of the path, on the deck of the ship that must face the storm and the sea. He who has called you shall not slumber; *he who keeps you will not slumber...The* LORD *is your keeper; the* LORD *is your shade,* so that the sun may not burn you. The things that try to make a slave out of your soul may not burn you. The Lord will protect you.

God the Lord, announcing Himself in the great thunder of Sinai, said to Moses during the Exodus, "He will protect you from all evil" (see Exod. 19:16ff.). The first evil is inside of me, weakness, contradiction, boredom: the heart that does not respond to the Voice that made it arise out of nothingness and called it to Himself. The other evil is those who surround you, the evil of society, the evil of the world.

But *he will keep your life. The* LORD *will keep your going out and your coming in,* the Lord will watch over you in your every step, *from this time forth and for evermore.* The source of the truth of life is not intelligence, neither ours nor our leaders', not intuition or fantasy, not the feelings of our heart. The truth of life is the voice that the Mystery makes in time and in space, the voice of Christ, preceded by the prophets and followed by that of the Church.

We can be witnesses by following the Lord, following Christ: abandoning ourselves to His story. "Can a woman forget her sucking child, that she should have no compassion on the son of her womb?" But "even should a woman forget her child, yet I will never forget you" (Isa. 49:15). This should be written along the walls of our room, in the town squares, on the mountains, everywhere: "I will never forget you."

40

YOUR CHILDREN WILL BE
LIKE OLIVE SHOOTS
Psalm 128

Blessed is every one who fears the LORD,
who walks in his ways!
You shall eat the fruit of the labor of your hands;
you shall be happy, and it shall be well with
*   you.*
Your wife will be like a fruitful vine within your
*   house;*
your children will be like olive shoots around
*   your table.*
Lo, thus shall the man be blessed who fears the
*   LORD.*
The LORD *bless you from Zion!*
May you see the prosperity of Jerusalem
all the days of your life!
May you see your children's children!
Peace be upon Israel!

We are living; therefore, we have arisen from the grave of nothingness. Our life is not an undefined stream, but a design.

May you see the prosperity of Jerusalem. Fruitfulness is sharing in the construction of this life, entering it to intensify the flow of life. The image of one's own life is the image of the Other; the image of one's own face is the image of another Face; the image of one's own creative energy is the image of that of the Other. We sacrifice our everyday self to this design for the authenticity of living, of creating, of being fruitful. Even the family, the fruitful relationship between a man and a woman, does not have within itself its own image. It does not have within itself its own measure, but the measure and the design to which man and woman must sacrifice what they were as they united. Indissolubility is the most acute symbol of the sacrifice to which a man and a woman who create a family are called; sacrifice is at the service of the design. The face of their relationship is not what they feel: it is the face of the Other, and the fruitfulness they have imagined is the creative modality of the Other.

Fount of life, source of humanity, source of the ultimate design of the world: fruitfulness is of Christ.

We have been called to the most radical form of fruitfulness.

41

But There Is Forgiveness with Thee
Psalm 130

Out of the depths I cry to thee, O LORD!
Lord, hear my voice!
Let thy ears be attentive
to the voice of my supplications!
If thou, O LORD, shouldst mark iniquities,
Lord, who could stand?
But there is forgiveness with thee,
that thou mayest be feared.
I wait for the LORD, my soul waits,
and in his word I hope;
my soul waits for the LORD
more than watchmen for the morning,
more than watchmen for the morning.
O Israel, hope in the LORD!
For with the LORD there is steadfast love,
and with him is plenteous redemption.

> *And he will redeem Israel*
> *from all his iniquities.*

Out of the depths I cry to thee, O LORD! This Psalm and Psalm 131 used to be sung by people climbing in pilgrimage to Jerusalem from all points of the Jewish Diaspora. The Exile was the symbol of the distance from the city of God, and thus the pilgrimage was a return to God: it had a penitential, Lenten, paschal significance (*Pasch,* in fact, means "passage"). It celebrated the return to the Lord in the awareness that the distance, undergone with suffering, reflects the situation of all in the universality of sin, their distance from the house of God.

If thou, O LORD, shouldst mark iniquities, Lord, who could stand? The cry to God starts with contrition, the confession of one's own evil. This is not necessarily sacramental confession; the recognition of sin is an indispensable preliminary condition for asking. The confession of sins fills one with fear of God, the acceptance and desire to depend on Him.

Forgiveness on God's part inspires fear in us much more than the justice that keeps accounts. It is His mercy that makes us truly dependent and orients us to conversion.

This is hope. *I wait for the LORD, my soul waits, and in His word I hope.* We are asking for help from the Lord. We ask Him for the ability to live the truth of ourselves, our total dependence on Him. <u>Our hope turns into certain and patient waiting</u>.

In the end *he will redeem Israel from all his iniquities:* His mercy and forgiveness, our confession and recognition of dependence on Him set us free. Sin has no more power over us. It no longer depresses us with its diabolical falseness, and being depressed over one's own sin is precisely the way to stay ensnared by the wickedness within us.

42

Like a Child Quieted
at Its Mother's Breast
Psalm 131

O LORD, my heart is not lifted up,
my eyes are not raised too high;
I do not occupy myself with things
too great and too marvelous for me.
But I have calmed and quieted my soul,
like a child quieted at its mother's breast;
like a child that is quieted is my soul.
O Israel, hope in the LORD
from this time forth and for evermore.

Psalm 131 brings the other side of contrition for sin
to the fore: the positive attitude of trust.

It suggests to us the attitude that we are called to
live: abandonment to the Lord to whom we belong
through our companionship with one another.

We are at the weakest point of our behavior when we begin with ourselves. But this posture ultimately wears thin, because it sinks into subjectivity.

Children are safe, content, and tranquil when they are near their mother and their father, even more so than when they feel strong and brave. And so the greatness of man lies in his living close to God, as a young man near his parents.

We cannot say "Our Father," except like a child quieted in his mother's arms.

If I live the breadth of gratitude, what awareness do I have of myself? I belong to what makes me grateful. My expression of gratitude is born from belonging to Christ, and the sign of Christ is our companionship, the encounters we have made.

We must have the heart of a child. Because we have to be children, let us pray to the Lord, who in the gesture in which He involves us — the Eucharistic Sacrament of the Mass — offers Himself with us to the Mystery who makes all things.

O Lord, help me to live like a child, with the heart of a child, so that I may more deeply penetrate the truth of reality, to announce the Gospel (the reality that is You), and to know You, the one, only, and true God, and Him whom You have sent, Jesus Christ.

43

I WILL NOT GIVE SLEEP TO MY EYES
Psalm 132

Remember, O LORD, in David's favor,
all the hardships he endured;
how he swore to the LORD
and vowed to the Mighty One of Jacob,
"I will not enter my house
or get into my bed;
I will not give sleep to my eyes
or slumber to my eyelids,
until I find a place for the LORD,
a dwelling place for the Mighty One of Jacob."
Lo, we heard of it in Ephrathah,
we found it in the fields of Jaar.
"Let us go to his dwelling place;
let us worship at his footstool!"
Arise, O LORD, and go to thy resting place,
thou and the ark of thy might.

Let thy priests be clothed with righteousness,
and let thy saints shout for joy.
For thy servant David's sake
do not turn away the face of thy anointed one.
                                          (Ps. 132:1–10)

Our life is not at the disposition of Him who has given us everything. Our life does not collaborate in making the entire world the dwelling place of God. *"I will no longer lie down, I will no longer be able to sleep until I have built the dwelling place of God in the world. I will no longer be able to enjoy my house, the comforts of my dwelling place, until I have built the dwelling place of God in the world,"* says King David.

This is the voice of a man laden with affection and charity. This is what the conversion of man to God is, conversion to the design of God: it is not being better; it is not a human perfection. Rather, it is the building of the *place for the* LORD. In this building man must totally forget himself; he must live his own being belonging to another thing.

The resurrection begins in our lives. New life is capacity for affection, for building the presence of Christ in all relationships where man's restlessness exists.

This is the great law of life: "Love Almighty God with your whole self and your neighbor as yourself: in this consists all the law" (see Matt. 22:37–40).

If the dynamic of building the dwelling place of God in the world fades, then our own whims choose a god; our comfort identifies or our presumption defines an idol.

Our life can be full of idols — not because our heart loves, gives itself, dedicates itself, or likes everything — but because it reduces everything to personal preference, a sense of taste, an interest, to limits that can be grasped, understood, and manipulated by us, with the illusion that we are a thing's owner. Our life can be full of idols if it reduces the limitless divine.

~~Sin is the reduction of God to one or another aspect of the human.~~

I will not enter my house or get into my bed; I will not give sleep to my eyes or slumber to my eyelids, until I find a place for the LORD, *a dwelling place for the Mighty One of Jacob.* When Charles Péguy went to Chartres, he saw the great basilica looming on the distant plain, which was then only a field. He wrote, "This is the place in the world where everything is recognized; both this old head and this fount of tears; and these two arms tempered by arms; the only corner of the earth where everything is contained."[1] So to David. <u>The dwelling place is where we find God, the path to our destiny. It is where everything in us is reborn.</u> *where do I find my dwelling place now?*

A *dwelling place* is the place where everything is for you, where nothing is against you, where everything is for your gladness, where everything is a sure path to the threshold of happiness and completion.

Bearing witness means creating a human reality where His power and glory are seen. The *dwelling place* is the point where I can see what all my life is looking for — seeing the power and the glory of God. Seeing! This is the design of the Mystery: It wants to make Itself known, to make Itself loved in human experience, time and space, in the years of our life. It wants to make Itself seen in Its power and in Its glory.

Charity is a willingness to work together to build this human reality, to build up His body in the world. <u>Charity is pure affection.</u> It is what Psalm 132 invites us to: I shall not sit down to eat and drink, I shall not put myself in the affectionate companionship of friends, I shall not go to rest, I shall not go to work, unless I have found a house for the Lord. *The dwelling place of the Mighty One of Jacob* in your person is an external dwelling place with which

---

1. Charles Péguy, "Preghiera di residenza," in *Lui è qui: Pagine scelte* (Milan: BUR, 1997), 387.

your person coincides. The dwelling place does not have an "inside of us" and an "outside of us." It is a single thing.

The fruit of our awareness of ourselves as belonging to God, to Christ, just as we are, is the capacity for affection: putting one's own person at the disposition of building the presence of Christ in the world, which is redemption. Fruitfulness is the capacity for charity, for loving in a wholly selfless way, entirely aware of the destiny of the other.

✱ What in my life builds this "dwelling place" and creates an awareness of myself to produce the "fruitfulness" being "entirely aware of the destiny of the other"? Am I living in this dwelling place? If not, should I be?

44

IF I FORGET YOU,
O JERUSALEM
Psalm 137

*By the waters of Babylon, there we sat down
    and wept,
when we remembered Zion.
On the willows there
we hung up our lyres.
For there our captors
required of us songs,
and our tormentors, mirth, saying,
"Sing us one of the songs of Zion!"
How shall we sing the LORD's song
in a foreign land?
If I forget you, O Jerusalem,
let my right hand wither!
Let my tongue cleave to the roof of my mouth,
if I do not remember you,*

> *if I do not set Jerusalem*
> *above my highest joy!*
>   (Ps. 137:1–6)

The song of the exiles tells us that while we suffer the grief of our human limitations, of our sin, of our hopelessness, there is one thread that can never fail. If we were without this thread, it would mean that we have destroyed our adherence to the covenant. And what is this thread? *By the waters of Babylon, there we sat down and wept, when we remembered Zion.... How shall we sing the* LORD'*s song in a foreign land? If I forget you, O Jerusalem, let my right hand wither! Let my tongue cleave to the roof of my mouth, if I do not remember you....* It is the image of the ultimate aspect of prayer, of the cry, the longing for the good.

Saint John says in his first letter, "God is greater than our hearts" (1 John 3:20). Even if we have sinned and our heart reproaches us, God is greater than our hearts.

"For God so loved the world that he gave his only Son, that whoever believes in him should not perish but have eternal life" (John 3:16).

45

THOU DIDST KNIT ME TOGETHER IN MY MOTHER'S WOMB
Psalm 139

O LORD, *thou hast searched me and known*
 me!
Thou knowest when I sit down and when I rise
 up;
thou discernest my thoughts from afar.
Thou searchest out my path and my lying down,
and art acquainted with all my ways.
Even before a word is on my tongue,
lo, O LORD, *thou knowest it altogether.*
Thou dost beset me behind and before,
and layest thy hand upon me.
Such knowledge is too wonderful for me;
it is high, I cannot attain it.
Whither shall I go from thy Spirit?
Or whither shall I flee from thy presence?
If I ascend to heaven, thou art there!

If I make my bed in Sheol,
thou art there!
If I take the wings of the morning
and dwell in the uttermost parts of the sea,
even there thy hand shall lead me,
and thy right hand shall hold me.
If I say, "Let only darkness cover me,
and the light about me be night,"
even the darkness is not dark to thee,
the night is bright as the day;
for darkness is as light with thee.
For thou didst form my inward parts,
thou didst knit me together in my mother's
    womb.
I praise thee, for thou art fearful and wonderful.
Wonderful are thy works!
Thou knowest me right well. (Ps. 139:1–14)

Let us try to feel within ourselves what the Blessed
Mother felt when she said, O LORD, *thou hast*
searched me and known me! Thou knowest when
I sit down and when I rise up; thou discernest my
thoughts from afar. Thou searchest out my path and
my lying down, and art acquainted with all my ways.
This vivid sense of belonging, which had become habitual in Mary and had determined the texture of
her thought and the substance of her feelings, could

certainly have been observed on her face, especially in certain moments. There is something permanent about those moments that point to the depth that the heart is familiar with. It is a serenity, a simplicity that inspires calm and gladness.

The depth her heart was familiar with made her capable of immediately perceiving the signs of what was being offered her. And so she said yes.

For all the discretion God takes to make Himself close to man, for all the delicacy with which the word of God makes Himself known to the heart of man, that knowing represents the acute, tenacious, and indestructible evidence of belonging to someone Other: *Whither shall I go from thy Spirit? Or whither shall I flee from thy presence? For thou didst form my inward parts, thou didst knit me together in my mother's womb.*

46

HIDE NOT THY FACE
FROM ME
Psalm 143

Hear my prayer, O LORD; give ear to my
supplications!
In thy faithfulness answer me, in thy
righteousness!
Enter not into judgment with thy servant;
for no man living is righteous before thee.
For the enemy has pursued me;
he has crushed my life to the ground;
he has made me sit in darkness like those long
dead.
Therefore my spirit faints within me;
my heart within me is appalled.
I remember the days of old,
I meditate on all that thou hast done;
I muse on what thy hands have wrought.
I stretch out my hands to thee;

my soul thirsts for thee like a parched land.
Make haste to answer me, O LORD!
My spirit fails!
Hide not thy face from me,
lest I be like those who go down to the Pit.
Let me hear in the morning of thy steadfast
     love,
for in thee I put my trust.
Teach me the way I should go,
for to thee I lift up my soul.
Deliver me, O LORD, from my enemies!
I have fled to thee for refuge!
Teach me to do thy will,
for thou art my God!
Let thy good spirit lead me
on a level path!
For thy name's sake, O LORD, preserve my life!
In thy righteousness bring me out of trouble!
                         (Ps. 143:1–11)

It is an exercise in wonder, of gratitude full of wonder, to repeat in front of Him, *I remember the days
of old, I meditate on all that thou hast done; I muse
on what thy hands have wrought.* The things of history and the things in my life are mine, the content
of my remembrance. Abraham and Isaac move me.
Moses is a figure in my life because the covenant is

a reality of my existence. Everything that has happened and everything that happens, everything from Abraham to Moses, from Homer to Shakespeare, everything has an echo in me, because all of reality is the complete horizon of my person.

There is no distance between me and ancient people, between me and Homer, between me and Dante, between me and everything that I study, between me and the nebulous ultimate, between me and the future, whatever it may be. No separation exists, because man has the capacity to stretch out his arms to embrace everything.

"Let us make man in our image, after our likeness" (Gen. 1:26). Man must reawaken to the awareness of his relationship with totality. Cardinal Newman said that when he was fourteen years old, he had the sudden perception walking down the street that only two beings existed self-evidently: God and the I.[1]

---

1. See John Henry Newman, *Apologia pro vita sua* (Milan: Jaca, 1995), 22.

47

THE LORD IS NEAR
TO ALL WHO CALL
UPON HIM
Psalm 145

The LORD upholds all who are falling,
and raises up all who are bowed down.
The eyes of all look to thee,
and thou givest them their food in due season.
Thou openest thy hand,
thou satisfiest the desire of every living thing.
The LORD is just in all his ways,
and kind in all his doings.
The LORD is near to all who call upon him,
to all who call upon him in truth.
He fulfils the desire of all who fear him,
he also hears their cry, and saves them.
The LORD preserves all who love him;
but all the wicked he will destroy.

> *My mouth will speak the praise of the* LORD,
> *and let all flesh bless his holy name for ever and*
>   *ever.* (Ps. 145:14–21)

Faithful is the Lord in all His words, *kind in all his doings*, because words and works are the same: I am word, His doing; the Lord is faithful to me.

The LORD *upholds all who are falling* [I am falling] *and raises all who are bowed down* [I am bowed down].

The eyes of all look to thee, and thou givest them their food in due season. Thou openest thy hand, thou satisfiest the desire of every living thing. The LORD *is just in all his ways, and kind in all his doings. The* LORD *is near to all who call upon him ... in truth.* [Whether one is seeking or not is a question as subtle as a steel blade.] *He fulfils the desire of all who fear him, he also hears their cry, and saves them. The* LORD *preserves all who love him; but all the wicked he will destroy* [the wicked are those who do not seek Him]. *My mouth will speak the praise of the* LORD, *and let all flesh bless his holy name for ever and ever.*

These words can seem unreal to us; but they are the most concrete reality. Yet for us they are abstract!

An agnostic philosopher was able to understand this. Wittgenstein said, "Christianity, I believe, is not a doctrine; it is not a theory of what was and of what will be of the human soul, but rather a description of a real event in the life of man."[1] A real event in the life of a real man pulls any doctrinal or theoretical category off its hinges.

---

1. Ludwig Wittgenstein, *Pensieri diversi* (Milan: Adelphi, 1988), 61.

48

HIS WORD RUNS SWIFTLY

Psalm 147

Praise the LORD, O Jerusalem!
Praise your God, O Zion!
For he strengthens the bars of your gates;
he blesses your sons within you.
He makes peace in your borders;
he fills you with the finest of the wheat.
He sends forth his command to the earth;
his word runs swiftly.
He gives snow like wool;
he scatters hoarfrost like ashes.
He casts forth his ice like morsels;
who can stand before his cold?
He sends forth his word, and melts them;
he makes his wind blow, and the waters flow.
He declares his word to Jacob,
his statutes and ordinances to Israel.

He has not dealt thus with any other nation;
they do not know his ordinances.
Praise the LORD! (Ps. 147:12–20)

Praise the LORD, O Jerusalem! Praise your God,
O Zion! For he strengthens the bars of your gates;
he blesses your sons within you. He makes peace in
your borders; he fills you with the finest of the wheat.
He sends forth his command to the earth; his word
runs swiftly.

Psalm 147 introduces us to the meditation on the
God who has come to work, to build His people,
those whom the Father has given into His hands to
build the glory of the Father in the history of the
world — that is, in the changing of our life.

He declares his word to Jacob: This event invades
our life if our life truly begins to share in His work. It
is a sharing in His working presence ("My Father is
working still, and I, man, am working" [John 5:17]).
The outcome of life as offering, action as a result,
awareness of belonging to Him, becomes a witness
that expresses His event.

One of the closing prayers of the liturgy says,
"May Your light, O God, guide us in every step of
life and grant us the ability to penetrate with a pure
gaze and a free heart the mystery in which You have

made us sharers."[1] The Mystery is God who has entered the world to sum up all things in Himself (see
Eph. 1:10), as Saint Paul said. Thus may He grant
that we be summed up in Him, that we penetrate
everything that we do with faith.

   The pure heart is the heart that is not centered on
self, and the free heart is the virginal possession of
people and things.

   Our relationship with God and with Christ is in the
event, that is, in the circumstance of the instant, now,
not a minute before or a minute after: loving being
in the instant, loving the living God in the instant,
loving Christ in the instant. The relationship with
Christ is in the instant!

   God has made Himself event, and "to penetrate
with a pure gaze and a free heart" is to live the
event; the circumstances; the instant; this contingent,
ephemeral, passing point of time and space; to live
it in the faith that is the recognition of the Presence,
adoration of the instant.

---

1. Prayer after Communion for the Solemnity of the Epiphany of
the Lord, according to the Ambrosian rite.

49

His Glory Is above Earth
Psalm 148

Praise the LORD!
Praise the LORD from the heavens,
praise him in the heights!
Praise him, all his angels,
praise him, all his host!
Praise him, sun and moon,
praise him, all you shining stars!
Praise him, you highest heavens,
and you waters above the heavens!
Let them praise the name of the LORD!
For he commanded and they were created.
And he established them for ever and ever;
he fixed their bounds which cannot be passed.
Praise the LORD from the earth,
you sea monsters and all deeps,
fire and hail, snow and frost,
stormy wind fulfilling his command!

Mountains and all hills,
fruit trees and all cedars!
Beasts and all cattle,
creeping things and flying birds!
Kings of the earth and all peoples,
princes and all rulers of the earth!
Young men and maidens together,
old men and children!
Let them praise the name of the LORD,
for his name alone is exalted;
his glory is above earth and heaven.
He has raised up a horn for his people,
praise for all his saints,
for the people of Israel who are near to him.
Praise the LORD!

Praise is God, *for all his saints.* Not for the one who is
faithful to Him, but for those to whom He is faithful,
for the *people . . . who are near to him.*

"Behold, I will open your graves, and raise you from
your graves" (Ezek. 37:12). The life we live every day
without perspective is, in fact, a grave, with the short
perspective of the corpse and the wall of the tomb.

We are led to a responsive relationship with the
mystery of God present.

Is the awareness of time that the morning stirs
in me a response? Between my eyes and the rest

of the world, between my heart and the rest of the world, there is nothing more serious than this: the relationship with the Mystery present.

As the light bears down upon our eyes as they open up in the morning, so His presence bears down upon our heart, upon our awareness, before any other thing. Through It, all things — each according to its form, each according to the attraction to our heart, each according to its entreaty for our help — will display themselves on the horizon of our life.

50

Thou Hast Cast All My Sins behind Thy Back
Isaiah

I said, In the noontide of my days
I must depart;
I am consigned to the gates of Sheol
for the rest of my years.
I said, I shall not see the Lord
in the land of the living;
I shall look upon man no more
among the inhabitants of the world.
My dwelling is plucked up and removed from
*   me*
like a shepherd's tent;
like a weaver I have rolled up my life;
he cuts me off from the loom;
from day to night thou dost bring me to an end;
I cry for help until morning;
like a lion he breaks all my bones;

from day to night thou dost bring me to an end.
Like a swallow or a crane I clamor,
I moan like a dove.
Thou hast held back my life
from the pit of destruction,
for thou hast cast all my sins
behind thy back.
For Sheol cannot thank thee,
death cannot praise thee;
those who go down to the pit cannot hope
for thy faithfulness.
The living, the living, he thanks thee,
as I do this day;
the father makes known to the children
thy faithfulness.
The LORD *will save me,*
and we will sing to stringed instruments
all the days of our life,
at the house of the LORD.

(Isa. 38:10–14, 17–20)

The Mystery — whom we are not capable of making
the cause of change in our days, in our months, in
our years, thus in our lives, in passages of time that
are too long in our life — we are compelled to feel
in the desolation of our soul. The Mystery coincides

with the inevitability of death, coincides with the inevitability of the limits of daily expression, of the passing hour. All is nothing. This is the word with which the Mystery informs all the situations of the I: all is nothing. We would live with this desolation at the depth of our heart if we were not freed by the distraction which is all things. We live with desolation because of our reflecting on what we are. The Mystery imposes Himself on us who forget Him; He imposes Himself on us as the inevitability of death. Were it not for the death of a companion, were it not for the death of a relative, of a person we know and care about, were it not for the death of someone close to us, were it not for the death of someone who in some way has crossed the path of our life, we would never think of death, while everything that is given to us is given to us for a responsibility that will have to be spoken, communicated, revealed, offered to God and the world in death. The Mystery compels us to think of Him when He shows Himself as death.

If we were every day shaken by the death of a person dear to us or by the death of something that really interests us, if we were shaken every day by death, then we would be different. Desolate, but different.

My dwelling is plucked up and removed from me like a shepherd's tent. When shepherds migrated, they rolled up their tents and threw them away, because they were useless rags by that time.

Only by thinking of death does something change in us.

"My father and my mother have forsaken me,"[1] and nobody takes me in. My eyes are full of tears, and nobody dries them for me.

Then suddenly, without your imagination being able to think of it, without your heart being able to need it...suddenly: *Thou hast held back my life from the pit of destruction, for thou hast cast all my sins behind thy back.* This Eternal Father casts all our sins behind His back. The principle of being, the wellspring of all things, the Mystery casts all our sins behind His back.

This gently changes our desolate situation. It is either nothingness or forgiveness, either nothingness or Christ.

The living, the living, he thanks thee. The *living* ...This is Baptism, when the death and resurrection of Christ cause me to be born again in a new life. In this way *the father makes known to the children* the faithfulness of His love.

---

1. Psalm 27:10. See text and commentary on page 29.

51

THIS IS MY GOD,
MY FATHER'S GOD
Exodus

I will sing to the LORD, for he has triumphed
    gloriously;
the horse and his rider he has thrown into the
    sea.
The LORD is my strength and my song,
and he has become my salvation;
this is my God, and I will praise him,
my father's God, and I will exalt him.
The LORD is a man of war.
the LORD is his name.
Pharaoh's chariots and his host he cast into the
    sea.
At the blast of thy nostrils the waters piled up,
the floods stood up in a heap;
the deeps congealed in the heart of the sea.
The enemy said, "I will pursue, I will overtake,

I will divide the spoil, my desire shall have its
    fill of them.
I will draw my sword, my hand shall destroy
    them."
Thou didst blow with thy wind,
the sea covered them;
they sank as lead in the mighty waters.
Who is like thee, O LORD, *among the gods?*
Who is like thee, majestic in holiness,
terrible in glorious deeds, doing wonders?
Thou didst stretch out thy right hand,
the earth swallowed them.
Thou hast led in thy steadfast love
the people whom thou hast redeemed,
thou hast guided them by thy strength to thy
    holy abode.
Thou wilt bring them in, and plant them on thy
    own mountain,
the place, O LORD, *which thou hast made for*
    thy abode,
the sanctuary, O LORD, *which thy hands have*
    established.
The LORD *will reign for ever and ever.*
                    (Exod. 15:1–4, 8–13, 17–18)

This is my God, and I will praise him, my father's
God, and I will exalt him: This is a sign pointing the

way. *My father's God* means the God of my history, of the history out of which I was born, not the god that I have chosen.

History is a struggle, and the Psalm contains images of struggle: *The* LORD *is a man of war....* *Pharaoh's chariots and his host he cast into the sea; at the blast of thy nostrils the waters piled up....The enemy said, "I destroy them."* Instead, with a single breath of Your mouth You covered them all up, You swept them all away; *they sank as lead in the mighty waters.*

Behold the wonder in which our sonship, our sense of veneration and adoration for the Father is expressed: *Who is like thee, majestic in holiness, terrible in glorious deeds?* This greatness is displayed in history: *Who is like thee, terrible in glorious deeds, doing wonders?* <u>Wonders are, in fact, a historical reality</u>: *Thou didst stretch out thy right hand, the earth swallowed them.*

The God of my history is a strong God who overcomes the entire struggle that is history, and generates wonder and adoration when we grasp the great works that He has accomplished and is accomplishing. *Thou hast led in thy steadfast love the people whom thou hast redeemed,* the people You chose for Yourself, among whom am I. You led them in Your steadfast love, placing Your strength at their service, Your strength which has conquered, the restless whirlwind of time. *Thou hast led in thy steadfast love the people whom thou hast redeemed, thou hast guided them by thy strength to thy holy abode.*

52

DO NOT SPURN US, FOR THY NAME'S SAKE
Jeremiah

Let my eyes run down with tears night and day,
and let them not cease,
for the virgin daughter of my people
is smitten with a great wound,
with a very grievous blow.
If I go out into the field,
behold, those slain by the sword!
And if I enter the city,
behold, the diseases of famine!
For both prophet and priest ply their trade
*   through the land,*
and have no knowledge.
Hast thou utterly rejected Judah?
Does thy soul loathe Zion?
Why hast thou smitten us
so that there is no healing for us?

> *We looked for peace, but no good came;*
> *for a time of healing, but behold, terror.*
> *We acknowledge our wickedness, O LORD,*
> *and the iniquity of our fathers,*
> *for we have sinned against thee.*
> *Do not spurn us, for thy name's sake;*
> *do not dishonor thy glorious throne;*
> *remember and do not break thy covenant*
> > *with us.* (Jer. 14:17–21)

Do not break thy covenant with us: Do not annul Your presence. But this is absurd! It is not possible! Saying *Do not spurn us, for thy name's sake* overcomes the great temptation to believe that it is impossible that God would maintain His covenant with a being like me, with beings like us. What is required of us is this certain entreaty, as certain as the child who abandons himself to those who gave him flesh and life: "Maintain Your covenant with us."

Since it is not possible for God's presence to disappear, we must also say, "Make us remember Your presence, make us witnesses of Your presence, make us watchful on Your presence," so as *not* to *dishonor thy glorious throne.*

This is the secret of our deep love for the reign of God. And so, "O Lord, do not break the covenant You have made with me!" are our truest words, the ones most appropriate to our days, which are often so wretched and foolish and devoid of fruit, that this is the only prayer. In fact, the Our Father says, "Thy kingdom come!" (Matt. 6:10; Luke 11:2).

53

To This People
Jeremiah

Woe is me, my mother, that you bore me,
a man of strife and contention to the whole
        land!
So let it be, O LORD, if I have not entreated
        thee for their good,
if I have not pleaded with thee on behalf of the
        enemy
in the time of trouble and in the time of distress!
In thy forbearance take me not away;
know that for thy sake I bear reproach.
Thy words were found, and I ate them,
and thy words became to me a joy
and the delight of my heart;
for I am called by thy name,
O LORD, God of hosts.
I did not sit in the company of merrymakers,
nor did I rejoice;

I sat alone, because thy hand was upon me,
for thou hadst filled me with indignation.
Why is my pain unceasing,
my wound incurable,
refusing to be healed?
Wilt thou be to me like a deceitful brook,
like waters that fail?
Therefore thus says the LORD:
"If you return, I will restore you,
and you shall stand before me.
If you utter what is precious, and not what is
        worthless,
you shall be as my mouth.
They shall turn to you,
but you shall not turn to them.
And I will make you to this people
a fortified wall of bronze;
they will fight against you,
but they shall not prevail over you,
for I am with you
to save you and deliver you, says the LORD.
I will deliver you out of the hand of the wicked,
and redeem you from the grasp of the ruthless."
                        (Jer. 15:10–11, 15–21)

Thy words were found, and I ate them, and thy
words became to me a joy . . . for I am called by thy

name. We received the word with avidity. We relished the experience of correspondence in the meaning of life. Yet it crashes against everything; and shame, alienation, or fury fill our relationships. It is a symptom that we need a strength that can only be invoked from the Spirit: "Come, Holy Spirit."

Why this contrast? Because the world lives and unwinds, and so does our existence, in a way that is contradictory to the word we received and the name that our being corresponds to. Original sin is a mysterious fact that will never be sufficiently borne in mind so as to explain man (not "the Christian man" but "man"). *Wilt thou be to me like a deceitful brook, like waters that fail? Therefore thus says the* LORD: *"If you return, I will restore you."* Behold in every moment the great possibility that His presence constantly reopens, because He is faithful to His love and His covenant. *If you return:* this is the drama of every instant, of every minute, the drama of our freedom.

Conclusion

Recognizing the Covenant

Mercy implies the object of mercy, which is why Christ the redeemer and I the sinner are, together, the gesture of the Father, the history of the Father in this world, the history of the mystery of the Trinity in this world. We are a single thing, a single Body, a single Presence.

"I am nothing but a creation of Your hands — not because You made me, but because You are making me. I am constantly formed on Your initiative. Give me light so that I may learn Your teachings."[1] The teachings of God are the facts of the covenant, and it is understanding and identifying ourselves with these facts that make us keepers of the law of God.

"He who meditates on the law of God day and night will bear fruit in due season" (see Ps. 1:2–3).

---

1. See Psalm 119:73. Text and commentary, page 126.

Catching the law of God in one's own life, identifying with a piece of the covenant is the life of Christian awareness. All our activity has no other value than to be seen as part of the covenant. There is no symptom more terrible than our distraction in the face of this.

The most acute difficulty is not in identifying all that we do with the covenant of God, but rather in identifying ourselves with the covenant of the Father, with the face of the Father, which is Christ. This "ourselves" does not exist except in the concrete pressures of the morning, the afternoon, or the evening, of the headache or the stomachache, of the thing that goes well or the thing that goes badly; all this is to make us identify with the face of Christ. I am no longer I; my name is the name of Christ who is mercy.

The only true balance is the balance of this identity. It is the balance of John the Apostle when he rested his head on the shoulder of Christ (see John 13:25). It is the balance of Saint Paul in the fourth and sixth chapters of the Second Letter to the Corinthians: "I have been beaten, and never conquered; I have been whipped and persecuted, and never brought down; I have been exhausted, and never finished off" (see 2 Cor. 4:8–9; 6:8–10).

It does not matter what level of perfection you reach. What others think or don't think of how much you do does not matter, nor does your judgment of yourself. All that matters is that mercy has taken you for ever, from the very origin of your existence. Mercy called you to love, because mercy loved you.

Holiness means always affirming — before everything else, in everything else — the embrace of the Father, the merciful, pitying movement of Christ, His gesture,[2] that is He Himself, independent of everything that stirs and has the appearance of life in us.

The word "covenant" describes and defines our entire existence, which is thus placed within the history of God in the world. The history of God in the world means the true activity of the world, because it is through God that the entire world is freed like yeast in flour, like a seed in the ground, even if no one is aware of it.

We must become more and more aware of God's covenant with us, of life as God's involvement with us, and therefore of the absolute and unmistakable importance, of the irrational influences of our outbursts, of our projects.

Nothingness, destruction, exile, is the life proper to the world, especially our life, without this covenant, which remains in me even in the destruction and in

---

2. See Isaiah 66:13: "As one whom his mother comforts, so I will comfort you."

the desolation caused by my wicked heart. Grace holds fast because God leads me to discover what He is and to understand that from my destruction He makes something new bud forth an identification with Him and the Father.

OF RELATED INTEREST

Lorenzo Albacete
GOD AT THE RITZ
Attraction to Infinity

A former NASA physicist and friend of Pope John Paul II offers a thoughtful, timely, and often whimsical look at why religion still matters. Albacete writes a column on religion for the *New York Times Sunday Magazine*

"*God at the Ritz* deals with the most awesome experiences of life. These experiences propel the human search for truth, beauty, justice, solidarity, and personal development. They confront us with the great Mystery that always lies beyond."   — *From the Introduction*

"Lorenzo Albacete is one of a kind, and so is *God at the Ritz*. The book, like the monsignor, crackles with humor, warmth, and intellectual excitement. Reading it is like having a stay-up-all-night, jump-out-of-your-chair, have-another-double-espresso marathon conversation with one of the world's most swashbuckling talkers. Conversation, heck — this is a papal bull session!"
— Hendrik Herzberg, *The New Yorker Magazine*

0-8245-1951-5, $19.95 hardcover

Also available in Spanish
Dios en el Ritz
0-8245-2113-7, $19.95 paperback

crossroad

ALSO BY LUIGI GIUSSANI

THE RISK OF EDUCATION
Discovering Our Ultimate Destiny

What does education consist of, and how does it take place? Giussani embraces our core as human beings and presents a fundamental guide for teachers and educators who are striving to understand the important role they have in educating the youth of today. Written from a Christian viewpoint, the book faithfully examines the rationale for education: how to educate ourselves, what education is, and how real education comes about.

0-8245-1899-3, $16.95 paperback

Please support your local bookstore,
or call 1-800-707-0670 for Customer Service.

For a free catalog, write us at

THE CROSSROAD PUBLISHING COMPANY
16 Penn Plaza, 481 Eighth Avenue
New York, NY 10001

Visit our website at
www.crossroadpublishing.com
All prices subject to change.

crossroad